Day Walks in Fort William & Glen Coe

20 routes in the Scottish Highlands

AF005898

Vertebrate Publishing, Sheffield
www.adventurebooks.com

Day Walks in Fort William & Glen Coe

20 routes in the Scottish Highlands

Helen & Paul Webster

Day Walks in Fort William & Glen Coe

20 routes in the Scottish Highlands

 First published in 2021 by **Vertebrate Publishing**. Reprinted in 2024.

Vertebrate Publishing, Omega Court, 352 Cemetery Road,
Sheffield S11 8FT, United Kingdom.
www.adventurebooks.com

Copyright © 2021 Helen and Paul Webster and Vertebrate Publishing Ltd.

Helen and Paul Webster have asserted their rights under the Copyright, Designs and Patents Act 1988 to be identified as authors of this work.

A CIP catalogue record for this book is available from the British Library.

ISBN 978-1-912560-64-6

All rights reserved. No part of this work covered by the copyright herein may be reproduced or used in any form or by any means — graphic, electronic, or mechanised, including photocopying, recording, taping, or information storage and retrieval systems – without the written permission of the publisher.

Front cover: Loch Leven and Loch Linnhe from the Pap of Glencoe (route 2).
Back cover: Corran (route 14).
Photography by **Paul and Helen Webster** unless otherwise credited.

All maps reproduced by permission of Ordnance Survey on behalf of The Controller of His Majesty's Stationery Office.
© Crown Copyright. AC0000809882

Design by Nathan Ryder, production by Cameron Bonser.
www.adventurebooks.com

Printed and bound in Europe by Latitude Press.
Vertebrate Publishing is committed to printing on paper from sustainable sources.

Every effort has been made to achieve accuracy of the information in this guidebook. The authors, publishers and copyright owners can take no responsibility for: loss or injury (including fatal) to persons; loss or damage to property or equipment; trespass, irresponsible behaviour or any other mishap that may be suffered as a result of following the route descriptions or advice offered in this guidebook. The inclusion of a track or path as part of a route, or otherwise recommended, in this guidebook does not guarantee that the track or path will remain a right of way. If conflict with landowners arises we advise that you act politely and leave by the shortest route available. If the matter needs to be taken further then please take it up with the relevant authority.

Contents

Introduction vii	Estate activities xii
About the walks viii	How to use this book xiii
Navigation viii	Maps, descriptions, distances xiv
GPS and mobile phones ix	Km/mile conversion chart xiv
Safety ix	Scottish place names xv
Bothies x	Fort William & Glen Coe Area Map xvi
Scottish outdoor access xi	

SECTION 1 – GLEN COE & GLEN ETIVE

1. The Two Lairigs – 15km/9.3miles 5
2. The Pap of Glencoe – 7km/4.4miles 11
3. Buachaille Etive Beag – 8km/5miles 15
4. Buachaille Etive Mòr* – 13km/8.1miles 19
5. Ben Starav – 16km/9.9miles 23

SECTION 2 – KINLOCHLEVEN & THE MAMORES

6. Blackwater Reservoir – 17.5km/10.9miles 33
7. Mam na Gualainn – 19.5km/12.1miles 39
8. Binnein Mòr & Na Gruagaichean – 13.6km/8.4miles 45
9. Stob Bàn & Mullach nan Coirean – 12.7km/7.9miles 51
10. An Steall & An Gearanach – 8.7km/5.4miles 57

SECTION 3 – FORT WILLIAM & THE GREAT GLEN

11. Cow Hill – 11km/6.8miles 65
12. Ben Nevis North Face – 11.4km/7.1miles 69
13. Beinn Bhàn – 8.3km/5.2miles 73
14. Sgùrr na h-Eanchainne & Druim na Sgriodain – 13.2km/8.2miles 77
15a. Ben Nevis by the Mountain Track – 15.8km/9.8miles 83
15b. Ben Nevis by the Càrn Mòr Dearg Arête – 17.8km/11.1miles 89
16. The Grey Corries – 21.1km/13.1miles 95

SECTION 4 – THE ROAD TO THE ISLES

17. Peanmeanach – 11.3km/7miles 105
18. Gulvain – 21.4km/13.3miles 109
19. Sgùrr Thuilm & Sgùrr nan Coireachan – 23.2km/14.4miles 113
20. Streap – 18.2km/11.3miles 119

APPENDIX 124

*Shortcut available

LOOKING ACROSS THE CORRAN NARROWS FROM DRUIM NA SGRÌODAIN

Introduction

For many people, the journey north on the A82 from Tyndrum for the first time is a memorable experience. The road climbs and climbs, then emerges on the vast, almost flat, watery expanse of Rannoch Moor. Continuing across this emptiness, the great pyramidal peak of Buachaille Etive Mòr comes into view, contrasting starkly and acting as a sentinel for Glen Coe. The road then descends into Scotland's most dramatic glen, hemmed between the towering walls of the Three Sisters and the jagged ridge of the Aonach Eagach. This is a landscape with a grandeur beyond anything to the south.

Emerging from Glen Coe the beautiful shores of Loch Leven are reached, extending right up to Kinlochleven at the foot of the Mamores. Beyond is Loch Linnhe, where the sea penetrates far inland, culminating at Fort William, the largest town in the West Highlands. Ben Nevis – the highest summit of them all – towers beyond, while beautiful Glen Nevis winds for miles into the mountains, a gateway to the stunning waterfall An Steall. To the north, the Road to the Isles leads to the dramatic monument at Glenfinnan, en route to a wonderful coast of sandy beaches and rocky bays.

It's no wonder that the region has called itself the Outdoor Capital of the UK. This is a walkers' wonderland par excellence. Here are imposing mountains with dramatic, airy ridges and precipitous crags; slender, winding sea lochs; atmospheric, brooding glens; towering waterfalls, and a convoluted, rocky coastline with deserted villages and a hidden history. This is a place whose secrets are best discovered by those on foot.

Be properly prepared though. This is an unforgiving landscape – the paths are rugged, sometimes boggy and sometimes nonexistent; the ascents can be demanding and arduous, while the weather is often wild. For those who treat this landscape with the respect that it deserves, the rewards are immense.

Helen & Paul Webster

About the walks
The walks in this book range between 4.4 and 14.4 miles (7 and 23.2 kilometres) and will take around three and a half to ten and a half hours at average walking speed without allowing for stops.

This is a rugged and mountainous region, and the walks reflect that. None of the walks are signed or waymarked throughout, so some map reading ability is essential. Be prepared for some pathless terrain requiring good navigation skills, particularly in poor weather. For the mountain walks, previous hillwalking experience is assumed.

Navigation
The Fort William and Glen Coe area is large and covered in full by a number of Ordnance Survey (OS) Explorer 1:25,000 or OS Landranger 1:50,000 maps, while Harvey produce two maps covering Ben Nevis, the Mamores and Grey Corries and also Glen Coe, Glen Etive and Black Mount in their 1:25,000 Superwalker range in addition to a 1:40,000 map covering Ben Nevis and Glen Coe in their British Mountain Maps range.

This book includes OS mapping as well as a route description; however, it is always recommended to carry the relevant map so that you can navigate to safety if you need to leave the intended route. You should also carry a compass and be able to navigate using it.

The routes in this book are covered by the following maps in the OS 1:25,000 Explorer series:
377 Loch Etive & Glen Orchy
384 Glen Coe & Glen Etive
391 Ardgour & Strontian
392 Ben Nevis & Fort William
398 Loch Morar & Mallaig
399 Loch Arkaig

GPS and mobile phones

A GPS and/or mobile phone with OS-quality mapping installed on the device can be very useful, both for pinpointing your exact position and for checking against a downloaded route. However, do not rely on having mobile phone signal and be aware that batteries can fail on long or cold days; carry back up batteries, leave phones in airplane mode to prolong battery life, and tell someone where you are going and when you plan to get back.

Safety

Well-fitting walking boots will provide the protection and grip your feet need on the mountain routes. Trail shoes may be adequate in dry conditions on the lower-level routes, although always prepare for some areas of wet ground. Similarly, always carry waterproofs, spare clothing including hat and gloves on mountain walks (even in the summer), food and drink, and consider taking a torch and first aid kit.

Sunscreen and a sun hat should be taken in the summer. Midges can be an annoyance during the high summer months, repellent and/or a midge-net are useful. The tiny insects prefer damp, still weather and can often be avoided by climbing high enough to catch a strong breeze and avoiding areas near placid water, particularly in the evening. Ticks, which can spread Lyme disease, are found in the Fort William area; carry a tick remover and check yourself at the end of the day. Long trousers and sleeves, light coloured clothing and avoiding walking through bracken are all good strategies. If you are bitten and then develop a 'bullseye' reaction at the bite spot, experience cold-like symptoms or feel unwell seek medical advice. **www.lymediseaseaction.org.uk**

Mountain weather can change rapidly. Always check the mountain weather forecast and be prepared for cold, windy and wet weather and know how to navigate in low cloud and fog. Sometimes the best decision can be to turn back – keep an eye on the weather and change plans if need be.

Winter conditions

The walks are described for summer conditions only. Winter mountain walking comes with its own challenges and dangers. The days are short; a headtorch and spare batteries should be part of your kit. When snow and icy conditions are forecast you must carry, and be adept in the use of, crampons and an ice axe. Check the Scottish Avalanche Information Service for current avalanche risks, plan your route accordingly and be prepared to change it. Navigation can be much harder when there are no paths visible on the ground. Attending a winter skills course is highly recommended, or at least go with more experienced people until you have the skills. Ensure that you have enough warm clothes and tell someone where you plan to go.

Rescue

In case of an emergency dial **999** and ask for **Police** and then **Mountain Rescue**. Where possible give a six-figure grid reference of your location or that of your casualty. If you don't have mobile reception try to attract the attention of others nearby. The standard distress signal is six short blasts on a whistle every minute.

Emergency rescue by SMS text

In the UK you can also contact the emergency services by SMS text – useful if you have low battery or intermittent signal. You need to register your phone first by texting **'register'** to **999** and then following the instructions in the reply. **Do it now** – it could save yours or someone else's life. **www.emergencysms.net**

Bothies

Bothies are unlocked shelters in remote locations throughout Scotland where hillwalkers, climbers and mountain bikers are able to spend the night. They range from rough stone shelters to disused cottages with several rooms. The Mountain Bothies Association is a registered charity taking care of around one hundred bothies across the UK. Visit **www.mountainbothies.org.uk** for more information.

Scottish outdoor access

Scotland's 'right to roam' law gives walkers rights of access over most land away from residential buildings. These rights come with responsibilities which are set out in the Scottish Outdoor Access Code (**www.outdooraccess-scotland.scot**) and summarised here.

Take personal responsibility for your own actions. You can do this by:
» caring for your own safety by recognising that the outdoors is a working environment and by taking account of natural hazards;
» taking special care if you are responsible for children as a parent, teacher or guide to ensure that they enjoy the outdoors responsibly and safely.

Respect people's privacy and peace of mind. You can do this by:
» using a path or track, if there is one, when you are close to a house or garden;
» if there is no path or track, by keeping a sensible distance from houses and avoiding ground that overlooks them from close by;
» taking care not to act in ways which might annoy or alarm people living in a house; and
» at night, taking extra care by keeping away from buildings where people might not be expecting to see anyone and by following paths and tracks.

Help land managers and others to work safely and effectively. You can do this by:
» not hindering a land management operation, by keeping a safe distance and following any reasonable advice from the land manager;
» following any precautions taken or reasonable recommendations made by the land manager, such as to avoid an area or route when hazardous operations, such as tree felling and crop spraying, are under way;
» checking to see what alternatives there are, such as neighbouring land, before entering a field of animals;
» never feeding farm animals;
» avoiding causing damage to crops by using paths or tracks, by going round the margins of the field, by going on any unsown ground or by considering alternative routes on neighbouring ground; and by
» leaving all gates as you find them.

Care for your environment. You can do this by:
» not intentionally or recklessly disturbing or destroying plants, birds and other animals, or geological features;
» following any voluntary agreements between land managers and recreation bodies;
» not damaging or disturbing cultural heritage sites;
» not causing any pollution and by taking all your litter away with you.

Keep your dog under proper control. You can do this by:
» never letting it worry or attack livestock;
» never taking it into a field where there are calves or lambs;
» keeping it on a short lead or under close control in fields where there are farm animals;
» if cattle react aggressively and move towards you, by keeping calm, letting the dog go and taking the shortest, safest route out of the field;
» keeping it on a short lead or under close control during the bird breeding season (usually April to July) in areas such as moorland, forests, grassland, loch shores and the seashore;
» picking up and removing any faeces if your dog defecates in a public open place.

Estate activities

Despite many people's objections on conservation and ethical grounds, shooting remains an important source of income for Highland estates and provides employment for rural communities. As part of exercising our right to access the countryside responsibly, we must take the interests of these landowners into account.

Red deer stalking season runs from 1 July to 20 October for stags, and from 21 October to 15 February for hinds. The majority of stalking that may affect hillwalkers is undertaken between August and October. Grouse shooting begins on 12 August, running until 10 December, with most activity earlier in the season.

Within this period, individual estates will have their own stalking times and locations, so please find out where stalking is taking place before planning your route. The Heading for the Scottish Hills scheme replaces the previous Hillphones scheme and provides up-to-date information on where and when stalking is taking place. Not all upland areas are included in the scheme: some sporting estates do not participate and in others stalking is absent. For more information please visit: **www.outdooraccess-scotland.scot**

How to use this book

This book should provide you with all of the information that you need for an enjoyable, trouble-free and successful walk. The following tips should also be of help:

1. We strongly recommend that you invest in the relevant maps listed on page viii. These are essential even if you are familiar with the area – you may need to cut short the walk or take an alternative route.

2. Choose your route. Consider the time you have available and the abilities/level of experience of all members of your party – then read the Safety section of this guide.

3. We recommend that you study the route description carefully before setting off. Cross-reference this with your map so that you've got a good sense of general orientation in case you need an escape route. Make sure that you are familiar with the symbols used on the maps.

4. Get out there and get walking!

THE MOUNTAIN TRACK ON BEN NEVIS

Maps, descriptions, distances

While every effort has been made to maintain accuracy within the maps and descriptions in this guidebook, we have had to process a vast amount of information and we are unable to guarantee that every single detail is correct. Please exercise caution if a direction appears at odds with the route on the map. If in doubt, a comparison between the route, the description and a quick cross-reference with your map (along with a bit of common sense) should help ensure that you're on the right track. Note that distances have been measured off the map, and map distances rarely coincide 100 per cent with distances on the ground. Please treat stated distances as a guideline only.

Ordnance Survey maps are the most commonly used, are easy to read and many people are happy using them. If you're not familiar with OS maps and are unsure of what the symbols mean, you can download a free OS 1:25,000 map legend from **www.ordnancesurvey.co.uk**

Here are a few of the symbols and abbreviations we use on the maps and in our directions:

 ROUTE STARTING POINT   ROUTE MARKER   SHORTCUT

 OPTIONAL ROUTE   ADDITIONAL GRID LINE NUMBERS TO AID NAVIGATION

Km/mile conversion chart

Metric to Imperial

1 kilometre [km]	1,000 m	0.6214 mile
1 metre [m]	100 cm	1.0936 yd
1 centimetre [cm]	10 mm	0.3937 in
1 millimetre [mm]		0.03937 in

Imperial to Metric

1 mile	1,760 yd	1.6093 km
1 yard [yd]	3 ft	0.9144 m
1 foot [ft]	12 in	0.3048 m
1 inch [in]		2.54 cm

Scottish place names

Many of the place names in the Fort William area and the words used to describe the landscape derive from the Gaelic language with a little Scots and Norse sometimes thrown in for good measure. Here is a short glossary of the some of the words you may encounter.

àirigh	shieling or summer shelter
allt	stream
baile	town or settlement
bàn/bhàn	white
beag	small
bealach	mountain pass, col or shoulder
bein/beinn	hill, mountain or peak
brae	slope
burn	stream
càrn/chàrn	stony hill
clais	gorge or ravine
cnoc	small hill or knoll
coire	corrie
creag	crag, rock or cliff
dearg	red
druim	ridge
dubh	black or dark
dun	fort
eas	waterfall
fada	long
fasgadh	shelter
fraoch	heather
glas	grey or green
làirig	pass or facing slope of hill
loch	lake
lochan	small lake
meall	rounded hill
meikle/mòr/mhòr	big
mullach	summit
òrd	cone-shaped hill
ruadh	red
sgurr/sgorr	peak
srath/strath	valley
stùc	pinnacle, peak
tigh/taigh	house

1	The Two Lairigs	5
2	The Pap of Glencoe	11
3	Buachaille Etive Beag	15
4	Buachaille Etive Mòr	19
5	Ben Starav	23
6	Blackwater Reservoir	33
7	Mam na Gualainn	39
8	Binnein Mòr & Na Gruagaichean	45
9	Stob Bàn & Mullach nan Coirean	51
10	An Steall & An Gearanach	57
11	Cow Hill	65
12	Ben Nevis North Face	69
13	Beinn Bhàn	73
14	Sgùrr na h-Eanchainne & Druim na Sgriodain	77
15a	Ben Nevis by the Mountain Track	83
15b	Ben Nevis by the Càrn Mòr Dearg Arête	89
16	The Grey Corries	95
17	Peanmeanach	105
18	Gulvain	109
19	Sgùrr Thuilm & Sgùrr nan Coireachan	113
20	Streap	119

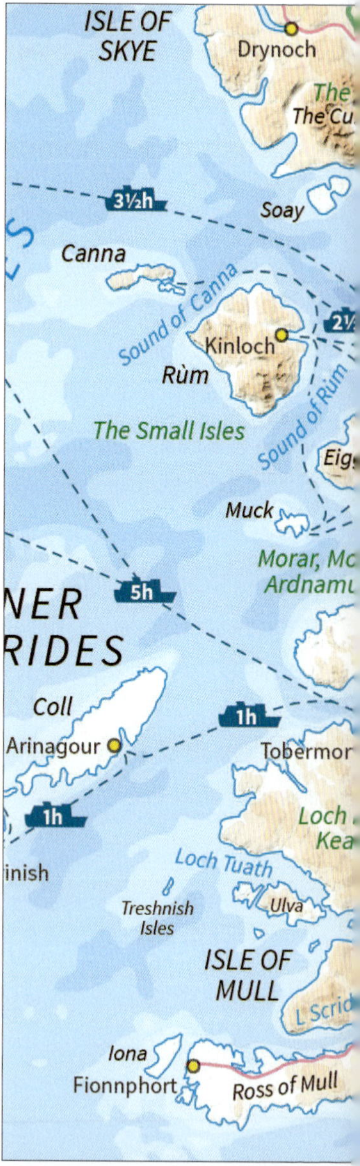

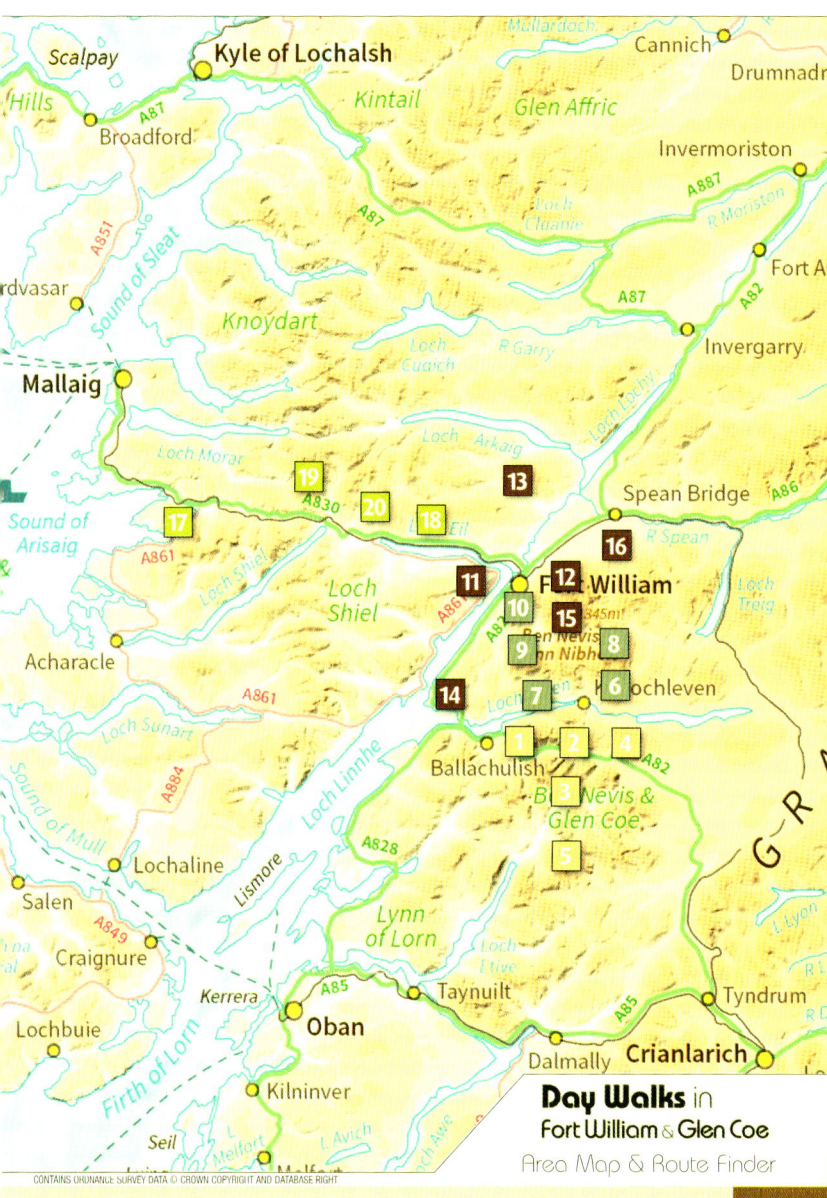

SECTION 1

Glen Coe & Glen Etive

Probably the most famous and possibly the most dramatic of all Scottish glens, Glen Coe's overpowering landscape is a perfect match for its dark history. It was here that the notorious massacre took place, with Campbell guests murdering their MacDonald hosts on government orders. To hillwalkers this is a true Mecca, epitomised by the great pyramid of Buachaille Etive Mòr, the guardian standing sentinel at the entrance to the glen, contrasting so starkly with the flatness of Rannoch Moor.

Just to the south, Glen Etive is much more secluded, threaded only by a slender ribbon of tarmac to the head of its namesake sea loch, rather than the thundering traffic through its neighbour. It is flanked by its own impressive mountain ranges, dominated by the great bulk of Ben Starav.

ON BEN STARAV

LOOKING DOWN GLEN ETIVE FROM BUACHAILLE ETIVE BEAG

THE BEEHIVE CAIRN, GLEN COE

01 The Two Lairigs — 15km/9.3miles

Link two historic passes on this circuit passing between some of the giants of Glen Coe.

A82 beehive cairn » Allt Lairig Eilde crossing » Lairig Eilde summit » Woodland gate above Glen Etive » Deer fence » Lairig Gartain summit » A82 » Telford's Road » Glen Coe » A82 beehive cairn

Start

Car park on the south side of the A82, opposite a beehive-shaped memorial cairn and a short distance above The Study. GR: NN 188562.

The Walk

The two lairigs are historic passes through the mountains between Glen Coe and Glen Etive. This walk combines both to make a circuit right around Buachaille Etive Beag – it's one of the few longer walks in the area that doesn't climb a mountain.

It starts by leaving Glen Coe to head south on a good path through the Lairig Eilde, whose name translates from the Gaelic as the 'pass of the hinds'. Once used as a coffin route, today it provides a secluded hike between the slopes of Buachaille Etive Beag and Bidean Nam Bian (the Three Sisters) on either side. During the initial climb the Allt Lairig Eilde is crossed on stepping stones. This is usually possible with dry feet although, like other crossings on this route, it may be impassable in spate.

Once over the high point of the pass the path becomes wetter as it descends towards Glen Etive. A fenced area of regenerating trees and scrub provides pause for thought on how this landscape might look if grazed more sustainably.

After crossing the burn the steep climb up to the second pass, the Lairig Gartain, begins; the name means the 'pass of the ticks' – you have been warned! The route is rough and boggy, but the views back down the length of the glen towards Loch Etive are ample reward. Eventually the sizable cairn marking the summit of the pass is reached.

From here the route descends the glen of the River Coupall to head back into Glen Coe. After crossing the modern A82, it picks up the remains of Thomas Telford's road through the glen, itself a replacement for the military road built to help subdue the Highlands after the Jacobite rebellions. Now a very wet and boggy path, it soon leads back to the beehive-shaped cairn opposite the start.

THE TWO LAIRIGS

DISTANCE: 15KM/9.3MILES » **TOTAL ASCENT:** 573M/1,880FT » **START GR:** NN 188562 » **TIME:** ALLOW 5.5 HOURS **SATNAV:** PH49 4HY » **MAP:** OS EXPLORER 384, GLEN COE & GLEN ETIVE, 1:25,000 » **REFRESHMENTS:** KINGSHOUSE HOTEL, GLEN COE, OR CAFE AT GLENCOE MOUNTAIN RESORT » **NAVIGATION:** STRAIGHTFORWARD BUT VERY REMOTE; RIVER CROSSING MAY BE IMPASSABLE AFTER HEAVY RAIN OR IN SPATE CONDITIONS.

DAY WALKS IN FORT WILLIAM & GLEN COE

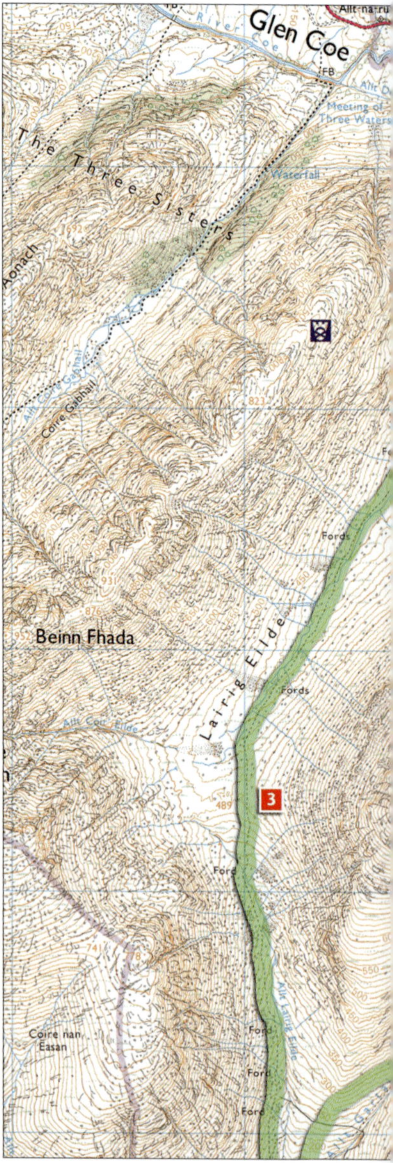

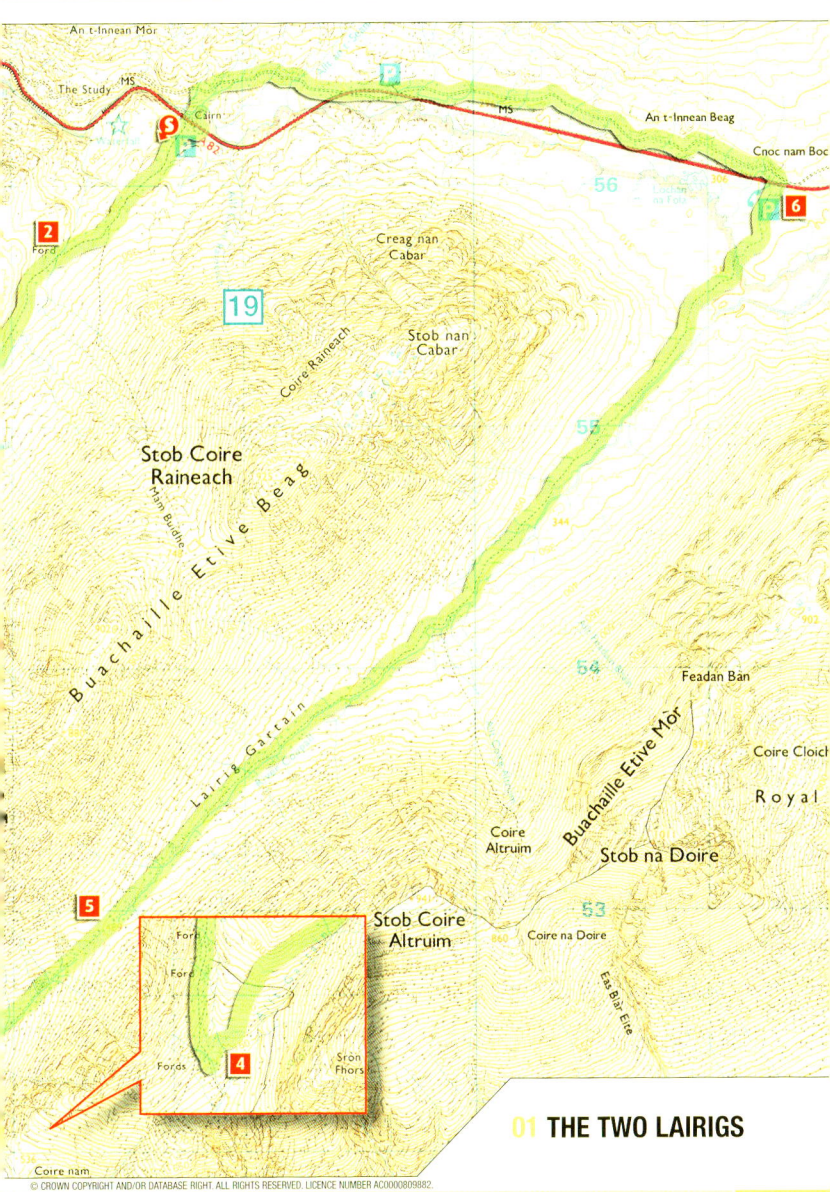

01 THE TWO LAIRIGS – **GLEN COE & GLEN ETIVE**

Directions – The Two Lairigs

1 From the car park **take the signposted path** towards the Lairig Eilde. At a fork **keep right** and soon the path slopes down and fords the Allt Lairig Eilde. This is usually a straightforward crossing on stepping stones; however, water levels can rise quickly and after very wet weather it may not be possible to cross. If this is the case turn back as there are similar crossings further on.

2 **Climb gently** on the clear path and after 1.7km **cross the stream** again. Continue up the southern side of the glen to eventually reach the summit of the Lairig Eilde.

3 The path now **descends, steeply in places**, with good views down to Glen Etive ahead. When a fenced enclosure is reached **stay on the path** to aim slightly right and **go through a gate** into the young woodland. At a path junction, just before two large fence posts, **turn left down steps**. At another junction **turn left** again and follow the path to the burn.

4 **Cross the water** and head along the very boggy path up the slope opposite. **Climb steeply** and **go through a kissing gate** after which the conditions underfoot improve as the route heads into the Lairig Gartain.

5 The summit of the pass – 489m above sea level – is marked by cairn. From here the route **descends gently,** staying on the north side of the River Coupall, following the wide glen hemmed in between the mountains of Buachaille Etive Mòr (meaning the 'big herdsman') and Buachaille Etive Beag (the 'small herdsman').

6 Eventually the path reaches the main road at a layby with a footpath sign. **Cross the busy A82** and take an indistinct path opposite. This quickly **swings left** and follows the line of Telford's Road through Glen Coe. These days this part of the 'road' is a spongy mass of bog myrtle and heather. Just before an old stone bridge is reached **turn left** to leave the old road and follow a path towards the beehive-shaped cairn. **Cross the road** to return to the start.

PATH INTO THE LAIRIG EILDE

LOCH LEVEN FROM THE PAP OF GLENCOE

02 **The Pap of Glencoe** 7km/4.4miles

The Pap of Glencoe is a celebrated local landmark giving a short but tough hillwalk with amazing summit views.

Parking near Glencoe village » Allt a' Mhuilinn » col » Pap of Glencoe » col » Allt a' Mhuilinn » Parking near Glencoe village

Start

Unmarked parking area on left, just after an electricity substation, 500 metres along the minor road towards the Clachaig Inn from Glencoe village. GR: NN 107588.

The Walk

Known in Gaelic as Sgorr na Ciche, the unmistakable cone of the Pap of Glencoe guards the lower entrance to Glen Coe, and is the final culmination of the Aonach Eagach ridge. For its modest altitude and the short distance, the Pap provides a much tougher hillwalk than many expect, but the rewards are tremendous. The summit gives awesome mountain and loch views in all directions, and there's a real satisfaction in looking at the Pap from the Ballachulish Bridge and knowing that you've made it to the top.

The walk starts just east of Glencoe village, following a path that runs parallel to a minor road. Once the climbing begins, at first on a track and then at a gentle angle on paths through young trees and open grazing land, the ground becomes much wetter underfoot. This is a popular route and erosion by feet and the weather has taken its toll; the path is very boggy and eroded in places, especially as the climb steepens.

Once the bealach between the Pap and Cnap Glas is reached the upper cone of the Pap is foreshortened and it looks easier than it is. The path heads up and around to the right and is steep, a little airy and very rocky, but involves only the simplest of scrambling. As it winds round to the far side of the Pap, the view all the way down Loch Leven is revealed – a fabulous moment. A final rocky slope leads up to the summit, a fantastic place to soak in the mountain, loch and sea views. The outward route is retraced back to the start.

If time allows, head up the minor road to sample a few drams at the legendary Clachaig Inn, a mecca for hillwalkers and climbers swapping mountain tales and planning new adventures.

THE PAP OF GLENCOE

DISTANCE: 7KM/4.4MILES » **TOTAL ASCENT:** 716M/2,349FT » **START GR:** NN 107588 » **TIME:** ALLOW 3.5 HOURS **SATNAV:** PH49 4HX » **MAP:** OS EXPLORER 384, GLEN COE & GLEN ETIVE, 1:25,000 » **REFRESHMENTS:** CRAFTS & THINGS, GLENCOE VILLAGE; CLACHAIG INN, GLEN COE » **NAVIGATION:** MAP READING SKILLS NEEDED; VERY ROUGH PATH WITH MINOR SCRAMBLE NEAR SUMMIT.

Directions – The Pap of Glencoe

1 From the parking area **take the Orbital Path to the left** as you face towards the road. After a while **rejoin the road**, ignore the gate signed *Laraichean* but **turn left** to go through the next gate. **Follow the track** and **go through another gate** and head uphill. Pass a bench with good views along Glen Coe. Just before a small waterworks **turn right** on to a wide path.

2 **Cross a footbridge** and traverse the slope of the hill, eventually crossing a stream. The path now narrows – **follow it as it bends left,** more directly uphill, keeping well above the steep ravine of the Allt a' Mhuilinn. The gradient relents at a couple of points, but these parts are the boggiest; the path is badly eroded. **Keep climbing up the path** as it steepens again on stony ground and **head diagonally right,** leaving the stream behind.

3 When it reaches 430m the path **turns left**, continuing uphill on wet ground. **Stay on the main path** when the path coming down from the Aonach Eagach ridge leaves to the right. Eventually the broad col between the Pap of Glencoe and its neighbouring peak Cnap Glas is reached. There are sweeping views down to Glen Coe with the Ballachulish Bridge and Loch Leven beyond.

OVER THE BALLACHULISH NARROWS FROM THE PAP OF GLENCOE

4 Cross the col to the base of the Pap from where the path becomes much rockier as it climbs steeply, aiming for the right flank. **Turn sharp left** following the path and then **bear diagonally right** as the path finds the easiest way through the rocks and boulders. Pass around the back of the summit cone from where spectacular views down Loch Leven towards Kinlochleven and the Mamores are revealed. From here take the final few steps up to the large summit cairn.

5 The return is by the **same route back to the col** and back down **the boggy path** all the way to the road. **Turn right** along the road and soon **turn right** again on to the Orbital Path to return to the parking area, or follow the Orbital Path all the way back to the bridge over the River Coe and on to Glencoe village.

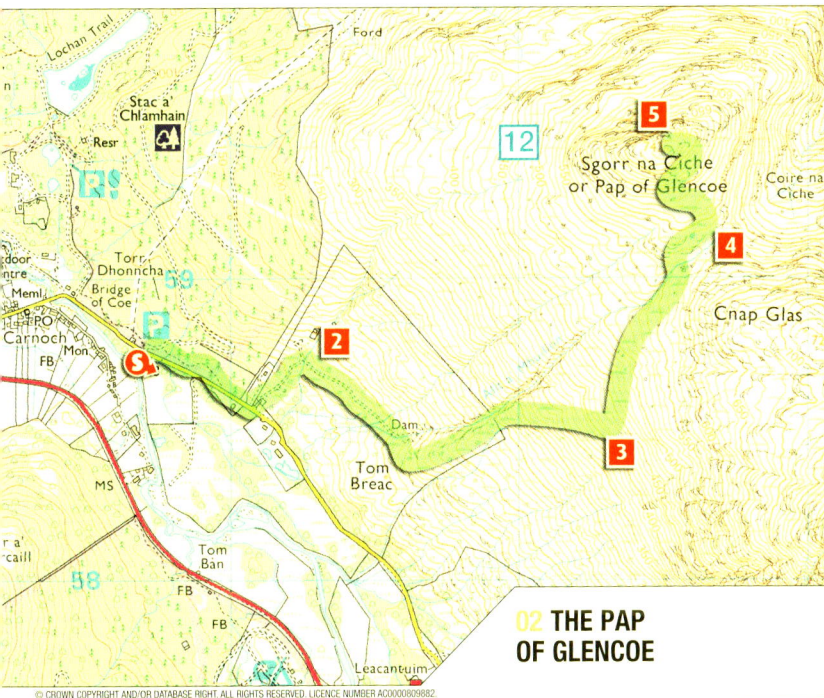

02 THE PAP OF GLENCOE

FROM THE BUACHAILLE ETIVE BEAG RIDGE

03 Buachaille Etive Beag

8km/5miles

The 'little herdsman' offers a dramatic ridge walk at the heart of an amazing landscape; a perfect introduction to the mountains of Glen Coe.

A82 beehive cairn » Mam Buidhe » Stob Dubh » Mam Buidhe » Stob Coire Raineach » Mam Buidhe » A82 beehive cairn

Start

Car park on the south side of the A82, opposite a beehive-shaped memorial cairn and a short distance above The Study. GR: NN 188562.

The Walk

The great steepness and rocky character of the mountains around Glen Coe has given them the reputation of offering some of Scotland's most challenging mountain walks. The wee Buachaille, however, offers a more straightforward ascent (in good weather) than its neighbours, while losing nothing in scenic grandeur. Starting from a car park just off the A82, the busy road is soon left behind as the route starts up an ancient right of way towards the Lairig Eilde, a pass linking Glen Coe to Glen Etive.

The real climbing of the day begins when this old route is left behind, turning up a path built by the National Trust for Scotland that takes a diagonal line up the flank of Stob Coire Raineach. In the autumn months this hillside echoes with the call of rutting deer stags. Steep rocky steps eventually lead up to reach the ridge of the mountain, at a bealach between its two major peaks – both of which are Munros.

From here a very fine ridge leads to the highest peak, Stob Dubh; although the ridge narrows and steepens, there are no difficulties. Stob Dubh – and especially the cairn just beyond it – enjoys a truly stunning view down the length of Glen Etive to its namesake loch, with the sea and islands beyond.

The ridge is retraced back to the bealach and beyond, following a faint path that leads up a steep and rocky final ascent to the second Munro, Stob Coire Raineach, a lookout point over Glen Coe. Finally the walk returns to the bealach once more to retrace the outward route back to the start.

BUACHAILLE ETIVE BEAG

DISTANCE: 8KM/5MILES » **TOTAL ASCENT:** 900M/2,953FT » **START GR:** NN 188562 » **TIME:** ALLOW 5 HOURS
SATNAV: PH49 4HY » **MAP:** OS EXPLORER 384, GLEN COE & GLEN ETIVE, 1:25,000 » **REFRESHMENTS:** KINGSHOUSE HOTEL, GLEN COE, OR CAFE AT GLENCOE MOUNTAIN RESORT » **NAVIGATION:** STRAIGHTFORWARD IN GOOD WEATHER.

Directions – Buachaille Etive Beag

1 **Take the path** that starts at the corner of the car park and immediately join and **bear left** along the ancient path leading towards the Lairig Eilde pass. This area and much of Glen Coe is now owned by the National Trust for Scotland and path repairs have greatly improved the going underfoot.

2 **After 500m keep left at a fork** to begin to head up towards the ridge. As height is gained there are great views of Bidean nam Bian and to the Aonach Eagach ridge on the far side of Glen Coe. **Stay on the path** as it leads diagonally up the slope. At around 400m it **aims more directly uphill**; a series of rocky steps aid steady progress. **Aim towards the lowest point on the ridge**, the Mam Buidhe. On the final climb to the bealach **fork right when the path splits** and **climb steeply** to reach the ridge.

3 There are great views both along the ridge, and down the far side into the Lairig Gartain, with Buachaille Etive Mòr beyond. **Bear right** along the ridge, climbing to the 902m spot height and continuing a dramatic traverse as the ridge narrows and heads towards the pyramidal peak of Stob Dubh. Despite the dramatic situation there are no difficulties in good conditions. **Climb the steep final pull to the summit,** which is marked with a cairn.

4 **Turn around** and retrace your steps back along the ridge to the Mam Buidhe. The path up to the second Munro, Stob Coire Raineach, is fainter and splits into several different variants. **Climb the rocky, steep ground ahead,** aiming directly for the summit cairn.

5 This is a superb vantage point over Glen Coe and Rannoch Moor with the remote Blackwater Reservoir also visible. **Retrace the route** back down to the Mam Buidhe. In poor visibility careful navigation is needed to ensure you are on the right route as a number of animal paths lead directly to the crags of the western slopes which need to be avoided. At the bealach **turn right** to head back down the rocky steps and back down to the Lairig Eilde. **Bear right** to return to the car park.

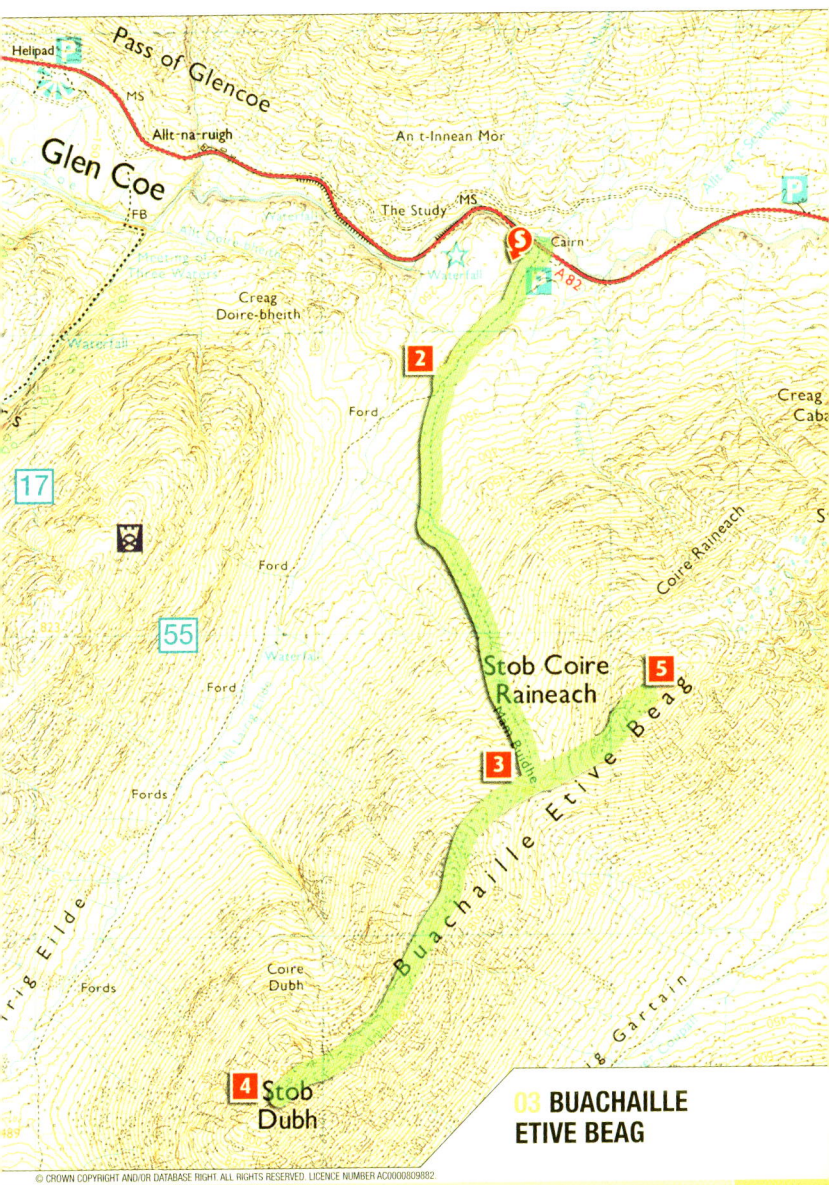

03 **BUACHAILLE ETIVE BEAG**

BLACKROCK COTTAGE

04 Buachaille Etive Mòr

13km/8.1 miles

An icon among Scottish mountains, the great herdsman of Etive may look impregnable but it offers a classic hillwalking day.

Altnafeadh » Allt Coire na Tulaich » Coire na Tulaich » Stob Dearg » Stob na Doire » Stob na Bròige » Lairig Gartain » Altnafeadh

Start
Altnafeadh lay-by, on the south side of the A82. GR: NN 221563.

The Walk
Buachaille Etive Mòr is the great pyramidal mountain that guards the entrance to Glen Coe, contrasting starkly with the flat expanse of Rannoch Moor. The forbidding face that presents itself to the road is only one end of a grand ridge of several summits, providing a challenging mountain day.

The ascent route up Coire na Tulaich can be seen from the rough parking area at Altnafeadh. In winter this is a serious mountaineering outing; the steep headwall is usually heavily corniced and has a reputation for avalanches. The corrie often holds snow into early summer – a trap for the unprepared.

The walk begins by heading to a footbridge over the River Coupall and then on to Lagangarbh. This is a private hut for members of the Scottish Mountaineering Club; the famed mountaineer Dougal Haston once redecorated the walls in the style of Jackson Pollock.

A stony path leads to the mountain, crossing the Allt Coire na Tulaich to begin the steep ascent, heading up between boulders and over scree before a very steep and loose final pull up to the ridge. From here it's a short walk to the main summit, Stob Dearg – an excellent vantage point looking down over Rannoch Moor, across which it casts a huge triangular shadow.

Buachaille Etive Mòr boasts not just Stob Dearg but a whole ridge of peaks, so the route retraces steps to the bealach before heading up the central peak, Stob na Doire. A superb ridgewalk continues down and onwards to end at the second Munro, Stob na Bròige, and a great view down Glen Etive. The ridge is retraced back to the last bealach before descending into Coire Altruim. There's some minor scrambling on the rough and rocky descent to gain the path through the Lairig Gartain which leads back to the start.

BUACHAILLE ETIVE MÒR
DISTANCE: 13KM/8.1MILES » **TOTAL ASCENT:** 1,110M/3,642FT » **START GR:** NN 221563 » **TIME:** ALLOW 8 HOURS **SATNAV:** PH49 4HY » **MAP:** OS EXPLORER 384, GLEN COE & GLEN ETIVE, 1:25,000 » **REFRESHMENTS:** KINGSHOUSE HOTEL, GLEN COE, OR CAFE AT GLENCOE MOUNTAIN RESORT » **NAVIGATION:** GOOD HILLWALKING AND NAVIGATION SKILLS NEEDED; IN SNOW COIRE NA TULAICH IS PARTICULARLY AVALANCHE PRONE.

Directions – Buachaille Etive Mòr

5➤ Start from the rough parking area on the south side of the A82 at Altnafeadh and **go straight ahead** on the track heading directly towards the mountain. **Cross the footbridge** and **bear right** to pass the Lagangarbh hut. At the next path junction fork right; the path starts to climb more steeply.

2 **Cross the Allt Coire na Tulaich** and keep on the path which climbs steadily up the side of the burn into the coire. As the route nears the top of the coire **bear right** on the path to weave through patches of boulders, keeping to the right of the central chute of scree. Further up the path **bears left** and soon picks a way up a small rocky rib before finally emerging on to the summit ridge.

3 **Turn left** along the broad ridge which narrows as the summit cairn of Stob Dearg is reached. This is the highest of the mountain's two Munros.

4 From the top, **retrace the route** back to the bealach and then **keep straight ahead** on the ridge, aiming for the intermediate peak of Stob na Doire at 1,011m. The route climbs and then **curves south** for the final climb to the summit.

5 Take care when leaving Stob na Doire in poor visibility, as navigation can be tricky here – leave the top heading **west-south-west** to follow the ridge down to the bealach. At the bealach **keep straight ahead** to climb up to Stob Coire Altruim.

  ➤ Shorten the route by missing out Stob na Bròige and descend instead from the bealach east of Stob Coire Altruim following the instructions in **7**.

  This section of ridge has steep flanks and wonderful views and is for many the highlight of the walk. **Keep heading along the ridge** to eventually reach the second Munro of the day, Stob na Bròige.

6 From the summit **return** along the ridge to the bealach east of Stob Coire Altruim.

7 **Turn left** to follow the path which descends northwards, staying on the west side of the Allt Coire Altruim. While the path is good at first, much further down there is a rocky section with a bit of scrambling, and some wet ground. Soon after this the floor of the glen is reached.

8 **Cross the burn** and **turn right** to follow the path along the Lairig Gartain. This leads back to the A82. The verge of this busy main road is followed for approximately 1km. **Turn right** and keep well off the tarmac, following a faint boggy path all the way back to the start at Altnafeadh.

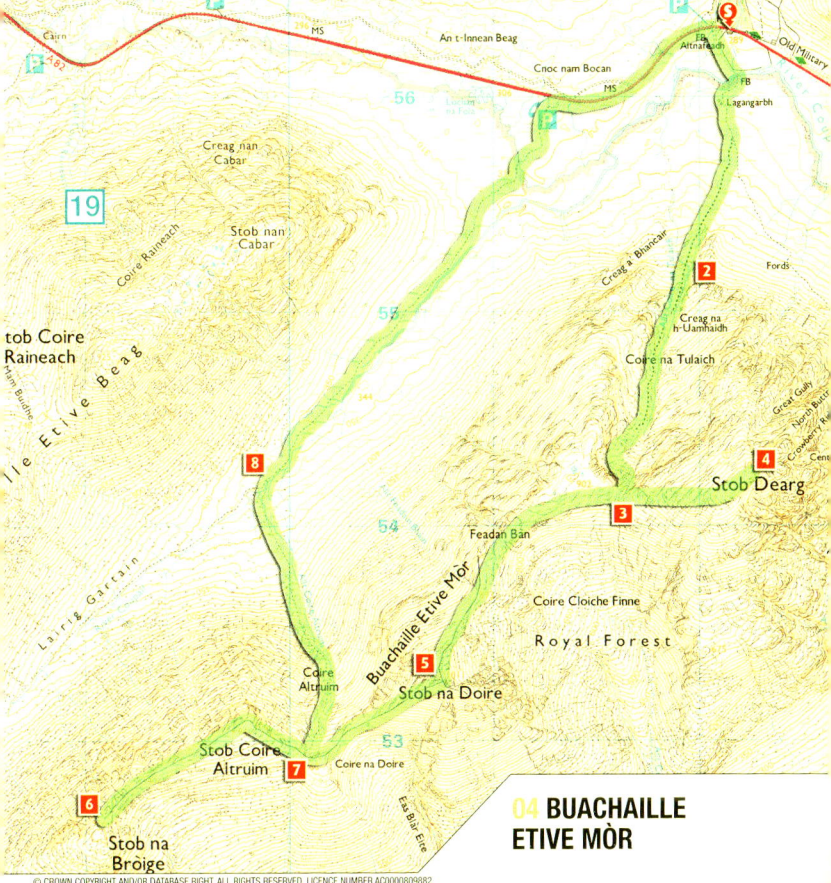

04 **BUACHAILLE ETIVE MÒR**

THE RIDGE TO STOB COIRE DHEIRG

05 Ben Starav

16km/9.9miles

Ben Starav rises magnificently from the head of Loch Etive, a mountain of great bulk yet with fine rocky ridges. It gives an excellent hillwalk in combination with its neighbour, Glas Bheinn Mhòr.

Glen Etive » Coileitir » Ben Starav » Stob Coire Dheirg » Meall nan Tri Tighearnan » Glas Bheinn Mhòr » Allt Mheuran » Coileitir » Glen Etive

Start

Parking towards the end of the road in Glen Etive, just east of the start of the track to Coileitir. GR: NN 137468.

The Walk

The journey down the winding strip of tarmac into Glen Etive is always a pleasure, and this pair of remote Munros is the finest outing in the glen. This strenuous day begins with an unrelenting and arduous direct ascent from sea level right to the summit of Ben Starav at 1,078 metres. Once this climb is over the rest of the route can be savoured, taking in some grand ridges including an airy rock arête that provides some optional easy scrambling. Best kept for a long summer's day, this route requires good navigation skills and experience.

In Gaelic Ben Starav means 'the hill of the rustling noise', which may refer to the autumn rutting of the red deer which can often be seen on both these hills as well as in the glen. Starting from near the foot of Glen Etive the walk crosses the River Etive at a popular wild swimming spot, bypasses a house at Coileitir and then crosses the Allt Mheuran to reach the foot of the mountain. The climb is steep and long, a demanding and relentless pull up Ben Starav's northern ridge. This eventually narrows to a satisfyingly rocky ridge before the steep final ascent – and a truly sensational view down Loch Etive.

The ridge walking just gets better as the route leads along a narrow rocky arête to Stob Coire Dheirg, before dropping to a broad bealach – where the walk could be shortened by heading down the glen of the Allt nam Meirleach. Continuing along the ridge the route rises again, proceeding along the tops to reach the second Munro of the day, Glas Bheinn Mhòr. From here the long descent is rewarded by views of the tumbling Allt Mheuran, perfect for a quick dip on a hot summer's day.

BEN STARAV

DISTANCE: 16KM/9.9MILES » **TOTAL ASCENT:** 1,423M/4,669FT » **START GR: NN 137468** » **TIME:** ALLOW 9 HOURS
SATNAV: PH49 4JA » **MAP:** OS EXPLORER 377, LOCH ETIVE & GLEN ORCHY, AND 384, GLEN COE & GLEN ETIVE, 1:25,000
REFRESHMENTS: KINGSHOUSE HOTEL, GLEN COE, OR CAFE AT GLENCOE MOUNTAIN RESORT » **NAVIGATION:** REMOTE AND STRENUOUS ROUTE REQUIRING GOOD NAVIGATION SKILLS AND MOUNTAIN EXPERIENCE.

LOCH ETIVE

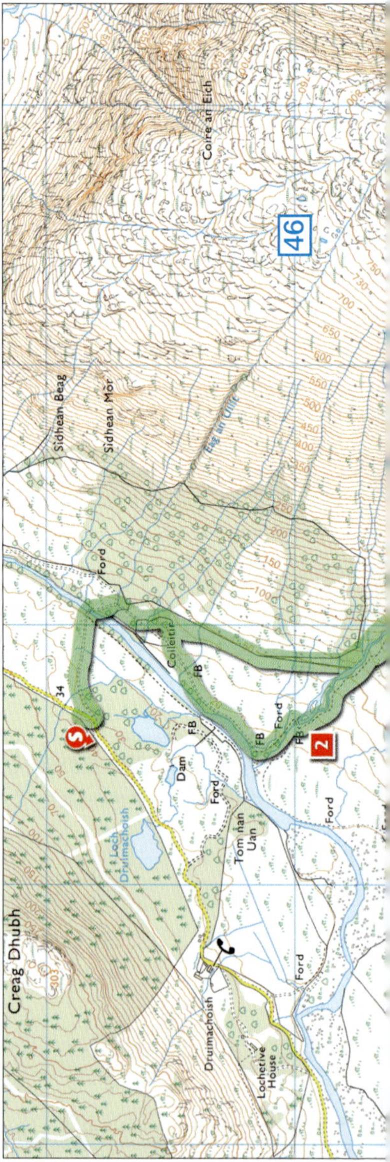

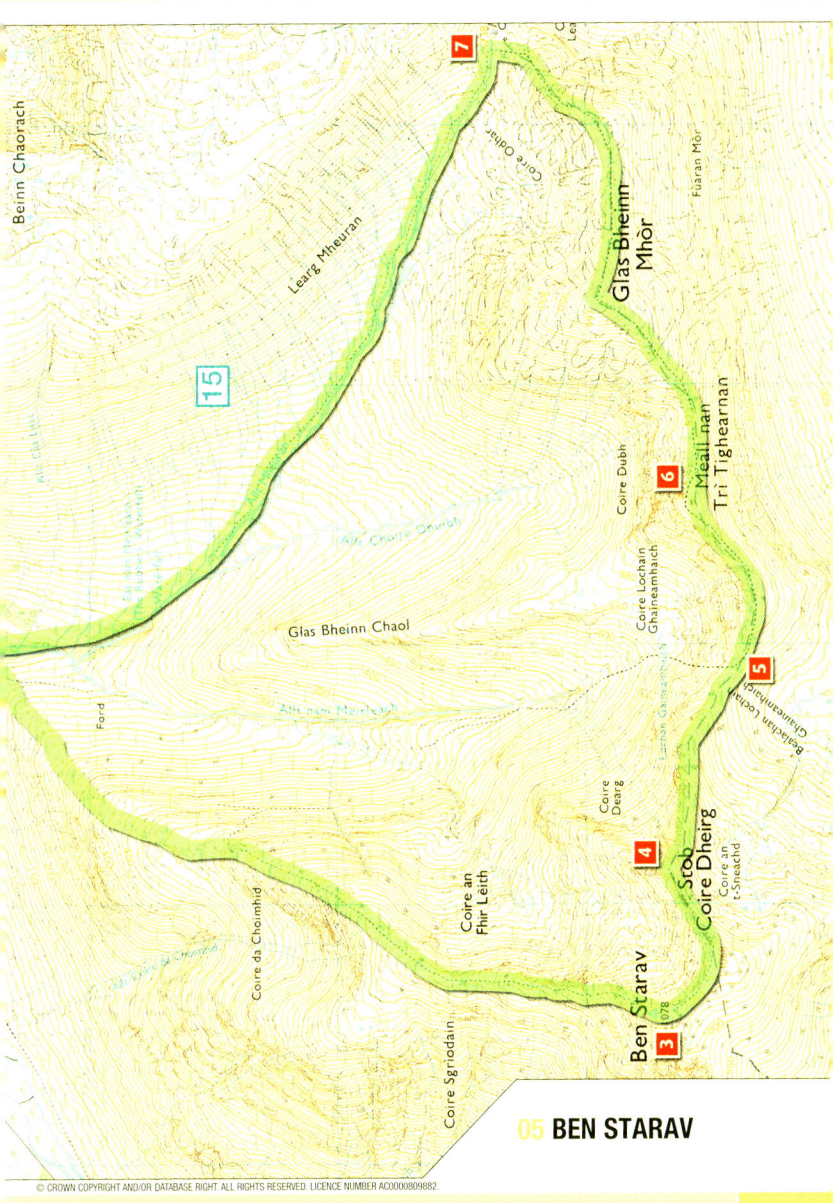

05 BEN STARAV – GLEN COE & GLEN ETIVE

Directions – Ben Starav

5 A narrow road winds down beautiful Glen Etive eventually reaching a track on the left leading to the river and Coileitir – this is the start of the walk. There are usually a few parking spots nearby and also about 400m further down the road; take care not to block entrances or the single-track road itself. **Return to the Coileitir track and walk along it. Cross the bridge** over the River Etive – the deep pool here makes a lovely spot for a refreshing dip on a hot day. **Keep right at a fork** and as you near the house **turn left** on to a boggy path which skirts round the edges of the grounds. Once beyond the property the path leads back to the track; **head left** along it. **Cross a small stream** on a bridge and soon reach the larger Allt Mheuran. **Turn left** and head upstream, soon crossing on a footbridge.

2 **Follow the path** by the Allt Mheuran for 500m. At this point **bear slightly right** on a rough path to begin to climb Ben Starav's north ridge. **Continue climbing southwest** up the steep slope, which is tough going and often wet underfoot. At around 450m the gradient eases and the ridge becomes narrower and rockier underfoot. **Stay on the path** which soon steepens again. At 800m the ridge combines with another from the north-west, and the ground levels off. **Stay on the ridge** as it bears south, undulating before it narrows. **Climb up the final rocky and bouldery slope** to reach the summit of Ben Starav.

3 The remains of a trig point and a large cairn marking the 1,078m summit provide a great area to enjoy the fabulous view of Loch Etive with the might of Ben Cruachan in the background. **Continue on the ridge** beyond the summit, curving round to reach the south-eastern summit at 1,068m. Take care to find the correct route from here, which **descends steeply** at first down the east-north-east ridge. When the ridge narrows to a rocky arête either **follow the crest**, which involves some easy scrambling, **or head slightly to the right** on a small bypass path. Soon the summit of Stob Coire Dheirg is reached.

4 Careful route finding is again needed here as the clear ridge heading north looks inviting but leads to crags. Instead **aim right to bear south-east** down another ridge, keeping the steep crags on your left. Rocky underfoot at first, the ridge broadens and becomes grassier as it descends to the bealach.

5 **Cross the shoulder** of Bealach an Lochain Ghaineamhaich and **bear east up the ridge** from here. A lovely section of ridge walking leads to a final climb to the top of Meall nan Tri Tighearnan.

6 **Stay on the ridge** and descend briefly before climbing to the 997m summit of Glas Bheinn Mhòr, the second Munro of the day. From here **take the path down the east ridge**, crossing grassy ground and bearing left before reaching the bealach at 738m.

7 **Bear left** to head west-north-west down the glen; **keep to the right of the Allt Mheuran**. Stay on the path which can be very boggy in places. There are some lovely pools and waterfalls on the descent. Ultimately the path returns to reach the bridge crossed earlier in the day. **Continue ahead and then bear right** to retrace the route to Coiletir, once again diverting around the back of the property, and **follow the track** back over the River Etive and up to the road.

CLIMBING BEN STARAV

SECTION 2

Kinlochleven & the Mamores

Formerly a centre for aluminium production, Kinlochleven enjoys an enviably beautiful location at the head of Loch Leven, and is now best known to walkers as a stopping point on the West Highland Way.

It's an ideal jumping off point for day walks into one of Scotland's finest mountain ranges, the Mamores, which can also be approached up scenic Glen Nevis on the north side. The Mamores include ten Munros, all linked by dramatic and, in places, airy ridges, and with a network of great stalkers' paths they can be climbed in many different combinations.

THE GRAVEYARD FOR THE BLACKWATER DAM NAVVIES

AN STEALL, GLEN NEVIS

FALLS ON THE RIVER LEVEN

06 Blackwater Reservoir

17.5km/10.9miles

A beautiful wooded glen leads to the bleak and lonely Blackwater Reservoir – a memorial to the toil of over 3,000 men who lived, worked and sometimes died in this wild spot.

Kinlochleven » West Highland Way » Allt na h-Eilde » Blackwater Reservoir » Cemetery » West Highland Way » Kinlochleven

Start

Car park off B863 Leven Road in Kinlochleven, just south of the Ice Factor. GR: NN 187618.

The Walk

The walk starts from the Ice Factor, housed in the massive buildings that were once home to the aluminum industry around which Kinlochleven was built. The first section follows the West Highland Way, Scotland's oldest long-distance walk and by far its most popular.

The route takes to quieter paths for the climb up through the beautifully wooded glen of the River Leven, passing a number of waterfalls. Higher up the landscape becomes more sombre as you arrive at open moorland. A giant water pipeline is reached, part of a huge hydroelectric scheme built to power the aluminum industry. A path by the pipeline leads to the imposing Blackwater Dam and the 13-kilometre-long reservoir behind it.

The route now descends below the huge dam wall down a series of massive, eroded concrete blocks. This requires a little care and agility but the close-up view gives an appreciation of the massive effort involved in its construction. The Blackwater Dam was one of the last major civil engineering projects built by hand. Labour was provided by over 3,000, mostly Irish, navvies who lived in a nearby encampment on the moor. Conditions were harsh and the living rough. A short detour leads to the lonely graveyard for the many workmen (and one woman) who perished during the works – a moving place. The harshness of life during the construction was recounted by one of the navvies, Patrick MacGill, in his semi-autobiographical book *Children of the Dead End*, which is well worth seeking out.

For the way back the route follows a track beside another hydroelectric pipeline, winding across the hillside before the long and twisting descent to Kinlochleven, with fabulous views en route.

BLACKWATER RESERVOIR

DISTANCE: 17.5KM/10.9MILES » **TOTAL ASCENT:** 550M/1,804FT » **START GR:** NN 187618 » **TIME:** ALLOW 6 HOURS
SATNAV: PH50 4RS » **MAP:** OS EXPLORER 384, GLEN COE & GLEN ETIVE, 1:25,000 » **REFRESHMENTS:** MO'S OR THE BOTHY BAR, KINLOCHLEVEN » **NAVIGATION:** STRAIGHTFORWARD BUT REMOTE, GO ADEQUATELY PREPARED.

Directions – Blackwater Reservoir

S→ Return to the main road from the car park then **turn right** to cross the River Leven. On the far side **turn right** on the West Highland Way and **follow the river upstream**. At a road **turn right** and follow it as it leaves the houses and becomes a track through woods. Soon **turn left** on to the signed *Ciaran Path*, leaving the West Highland Way to climb steeply. **Turn right** at a T-junction on to a larger path which climbs up through the beautiful glen. **Head straight across a track** to continue up the flank of the glen high above the river. Much of the water has been diverted into the hydroelectric power works originally built to power the aluminium smelters.

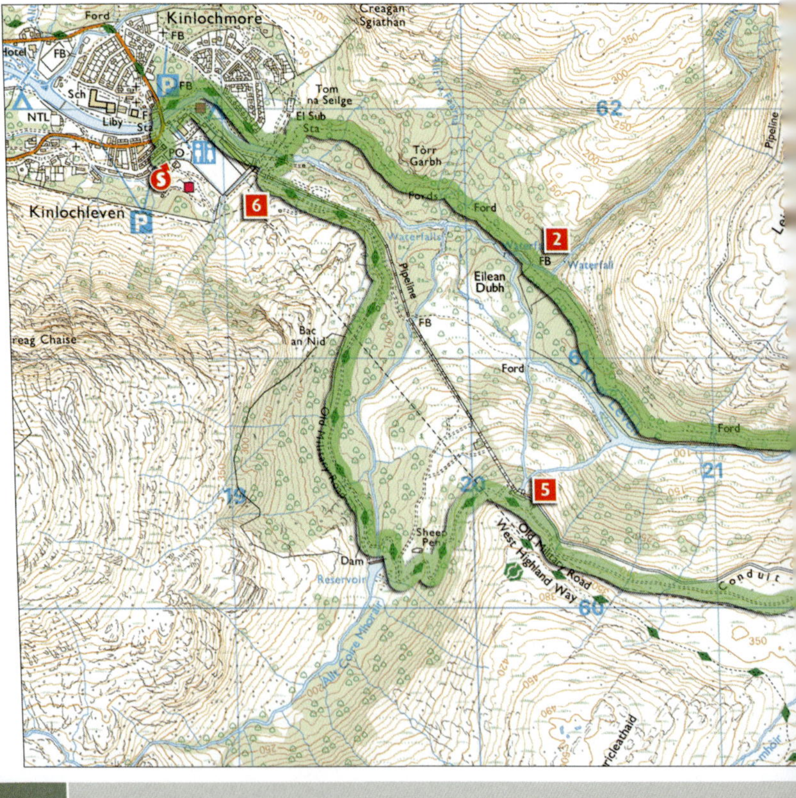

2 **Cross a wooden footbridge,** soon passing a waterfall on your left. The concrete ruins half hidden among the trees further on are what remains of a camp used to house German prisoners of war during World War I. The prisoners were put to work on the hydroelectric pipeline and nearby road building. Continue on the path, crossing the Allt na Duibhe below another waterfall. The going becomes rough and the path crosses another burn – it's best to cross a little above the ruinous bridge. The woodland is now left behind and the path crosses open moorland, boggy in places.

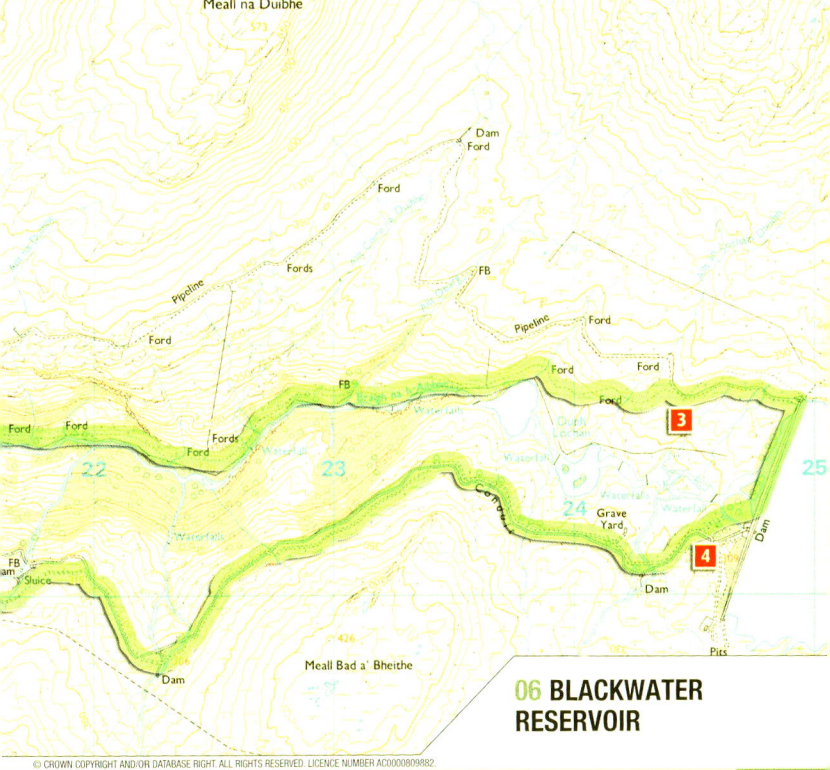

06 BLACKWATER RESERVOIR

06 BLACKWATER RESERVOIR – **KINLOCHLEVEN & THE MAMORES**

Directions – Blackwater Reservoir continued...

3 Eventually the hydroelectric pipeline is reached. **Turn right** to follow the path alongside the pipe to reach the north end of Blackwater Dam, an impressive structure holding back the waters of the 13km-long reservoir. Completed in 1909, the dam was one of the last big engineering projects to be built by hand without the aid of mechanised earth-moving machinery. The top of the dam wall is out of bounds so it is necessary to cross to the far side by descending along the base of the vast concrete wall. **Carefully descend the huge, rough concrete blocks**; the scale of the dam above is intimidating. Just beyond the halfway point **climb up to reach a fence** enclosing the outfall, then **turn right** along the fence and when it turns left **keep straight ahead** on a rough path to reach a crossing point over the burn. Follow a stony track on the far side and arrive at a T-junction.

4 **Turn right** at the T-junction on to another track heading away from the dam. The track follows a set of pipes carrying water to the hydroelectric power plant in Kinlochleven which is still in use today. Look out for the fenced cemetery sited on a small hillock on the right – the last resting place of many of the navvies who died during the construction of the dam. It's a poignant spot and well worth exploring. **Continue along the track** for another 5km, enjoying excellent views of the Mamores.

5 Eventually the West Highland Way is joined and you're likely to encounter groups of walkers making their way down to Kinlochleven, having climbed over the Devil's Staircase at the entrance to Glen Coe. This pass claimed the lives of a number of dam workers, some of whom perished in deep snow trying to return from the Kingshouse pub located on the far side of the Devil's Staircase. At the end of the concrete culvert is a cluster of buildings. Pass these and **stay on the track**. From here the water pipes head steeply downhill providing the huge amount of power once needed to power the aluminum smelter. The track takes a much more gentle and deceptively long route back down, with zigzags; there are soon fabulous views over Kinlochleven below.

6 Near the bottom of the glen **cross a bridge** over the pipes and **turn left** alongside the river, soon passing the Blackwater Hostel and old aluminum factory to return to the car park.

THE BLACKWATER DAM

HEADING UP BEINN NA CAILLICH

07 Mam na Gualainn

19.5km/12.1miles

This unfairly neglected hill provides a splendid grassy ridgewalk high above Loch Leven, combined with a section of the West Highland Way to make a superb circuit.

Kinlochleven » West Highland Way » Beinn na Caillich » Mam na Gualainn » Lairigmòr » West Highland Way » Kinlochleven

Start

Grey Mares Tail car park (parking charge), adjacent to St Paul's Church, Kinlochleven. GR: NN 188622.

The Walk

Having lost its aluminium industry, Kinlochleven has taken advantage of its splendid location to reinvent itself as a base for walkers heading into the mountains, and a pitstop on the West Highland Way. This walk begins along the Way towards Fort William, with an initial climb through beautiful woodland. However it's not until the Way and its huddles of overburdened hikers are left behind that the walk drops down to cross a burn and the real ascent begins.

There's a steep climb up the nose of the ridge, relenting briefly before the ascent up to reach the summit of the first and most dramatic peak on the ridge, Beinn na Caillich – 'the hill of the old woman'. From here the next section is a sheer delight, a grassy ridge walk above slopes that plunge dramatically down to Loch Leven on your left. Beyond a col the ridge climbs and broadens before continuing up to the summit cairn of the higher peak, Mam na Gualainn, a welcome backrest from which to survey the great view of Beinn a' Bheithir with the sea and islands beyond. Mam na Gualainn is a Corbett – a Scottish mountain between 2,500 and 3,000 feet in height with 500 feet of descent on all sides; bagging Corbetts is becoming increasingly popular as more hillwalkers begin to look beyond the better-known Munros.

The descent is rough and pathless at first, boggy in places, but eventually the old path from Callert is joined. This leads down to the ruins at Lairigmòr. Here the West Highland Way is rejoined; Lairigmòr means 'great pass' and the route climbs briefly, passing more ruins in the shadow of the great Mamore mountain range. Now all is downhill as the West Highland Way is followed down the glen of the Allt Nathrach for the return to Kinlochleven.

MAM NA GUALAINN

DISTANCE: 19.5KM/12.1MILES » **TOTAL ASCENT:** 1,084M/3,556FT » **START** GR: NN 188622 » **TIME:** ALLOW 7.5 HOURS **SATNAV:** PH50 4QT » **MAP:** OS EXPLORER 392, BEN NEVIS & FORT WILLIAM, 1:25,000 » **REFRESHMENTS:** MO'S OR THE BOTHY BAR, KINLOCHLEVEN » **NAVIGATION:** STRAIGHTFORWARD HILLWALK, GOOD NAVIGATION SKILLS NEEDED IN POOR CONDITIONS.

Directions – Mam na Gualainn

1 Beginning from the car park beside St Paul's church in Kinlochleven, **turn right** on to Wades Road. At the main road (B863) **turn right** and continue until opposite the football pitch. **Turn right** on to the West Highland Way and climb through birchwoods. At a fork **branch left** and soon **head straight across a road** to continue up the footpath. **Bear right** when another path joins, and pass a viewpoint overlooking Kinlochleven. At a track **turn left** to continue along the West Highland Way – usually from this point walkers are on a final long day heading to Fort William.

2 After 1km on the track **turn left on to a small path** downhill. **Go through the gate and cross a footbridge** over the Allt Nathrach. Now **start climbing** towards Beinn na Caillich; as the path gets steeper there are zigzags and good views over the nearby Mamores. At around 460m the going becomes less steep; before the path steepens again **bear right of the peak** ahead. The ridge is reached just beyond an initial cairn; follow the ridge to reach the summit of Beinn na Caillich at 764m.

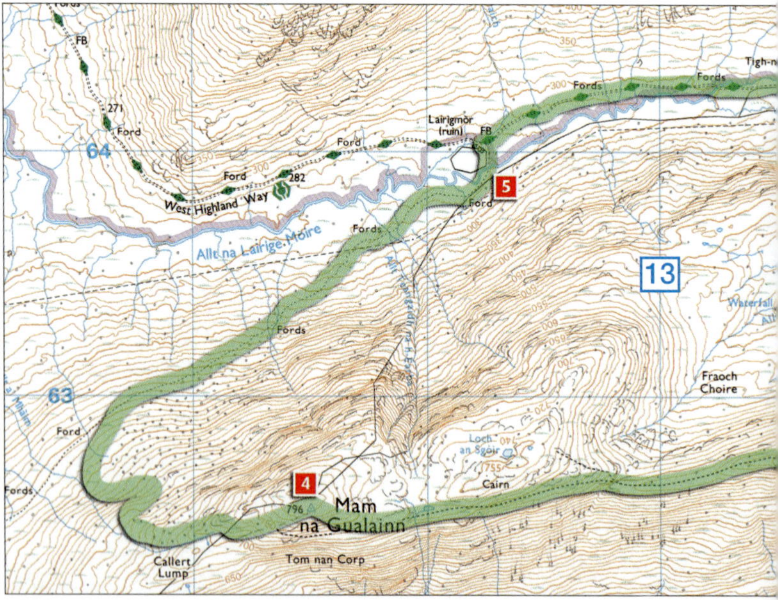

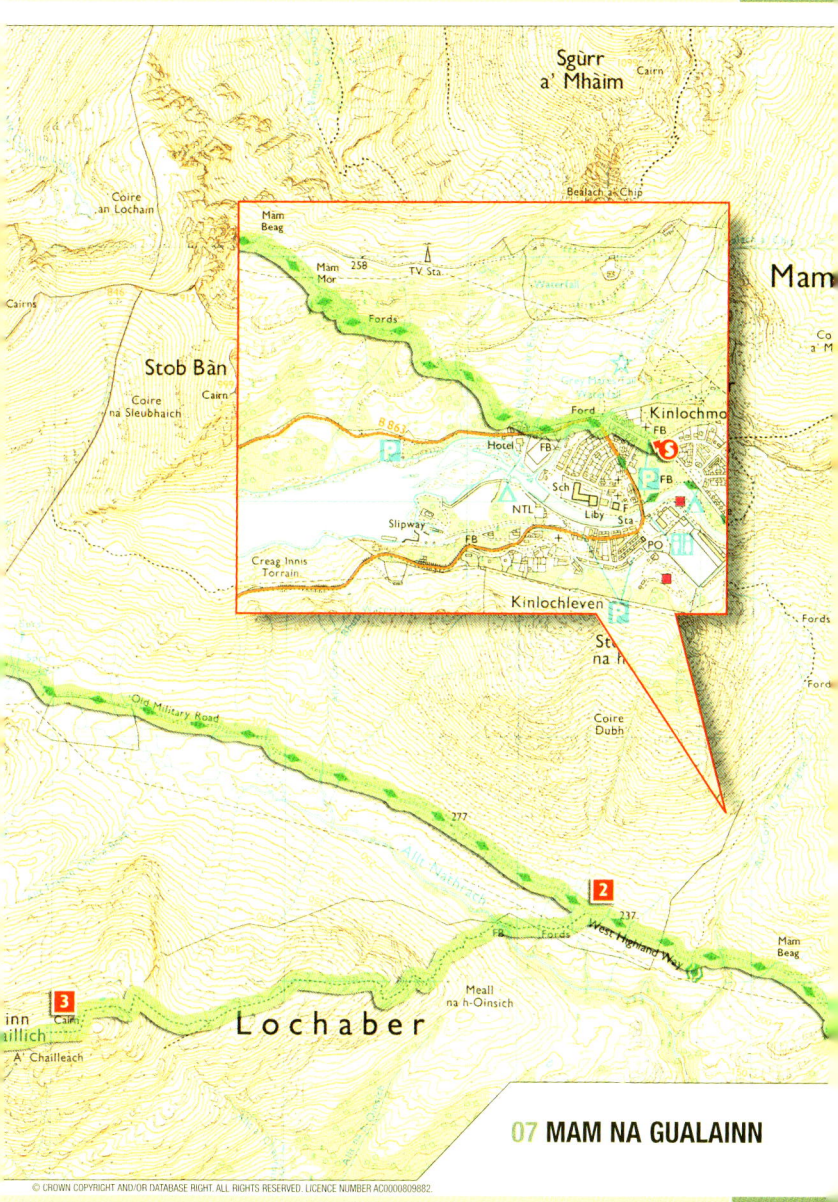

07 **MAM NA GUALAINN**

Directions – Mam na Gualainn continued...

3 **Keep heading along the ridge** for a lovely walk with good going underfoot and superb views of Loch Leven to the left and the mountains and seascapes all around. **Cross a bealach;** after this the ridge broadens and passes a minor summit at 755m. Keep heading along the ridge now on pathless terrain. **Cross another dip and climb to the summit cairn** and trig point of Mam na Gualainn.

4 At 796m this mountain is classed as a Corbett; although these hills are gaining in popularity it remains a place where you are likely to be alone at the summit to drink in the spectacular views. **Keep to the left** of the fence to **descend the ridge** ahead. Soon **follow a path through a gate. Bear slightly right** from here, again on pathless ground, **aiming to the right of a depression** at the head of a stream, north of the ridge marked Callert Lump on the map. Further down there are traces of an old stalking path, **follow these** to eventually meet the clearer path crossing the pass from Callert. **Turn right** and descend the path which is boggy in places.

5 Once down in the glen the Allt na Lairige Mòire is reached opposite the ruined cottage at Lairigmòr. **Cross on stepping stones**, which is usually straightforward – in very high spate conditions it may be necessary to stay on the southern side of the river and head east along the riverbank for 1km to pick up the West Highland Way near Tigh-na-sleubhaich. At the track **turn right,** now following the West Highland Way all the way back to Kinlochleven. Pass the old building at Tigh-na-sleubhaich and follow the outward route to descend to the B863. **Turn left and then left again after the bridge** into Wades Road to return to the start.

ON THE MAM NA GUALAINN RIDGE

LOCH LEVEN FROM THE SLOPES OF NA GRUAGAICHEAN

08 Binnein Mòr & Na Gruagaichean   13.6km/8.4miles

The towering and slender summit ridge of Binnein Mòr is a fitting high point for the Mamores, one of Scotland's finest mountain ranges. Combined with Na Gruagaichean it makes a fantastic though challenging hillwalk.

Kinlochleven » An Cumhann » Sgòr Eilde Beag » Binnein Mòr » Na Gruagaichean » Leachd na h-Aire » Kinlochleven

Start
Grey Mares Tail car park (parking charge), adjacent to St Paul's Church, Kinlochleven. GR: NN 188622.

The Walk
Kinlochleven provides a sea-level start for this classic mountain day. The route begins from the car park for the Grey Mares Tail. The initial climb is through mixed woodland, soon steepening and eventually emerging above the trees. The effort is rewarded with a classic view back down the length of Loch Leven, with the Pap of Glencoe prominent.

The Mamores have a range of superb old stalkers' paths and full use is made of them on the approach, following one such path for the ascent of the southern flank of Sgòr Eilde Beag, utilising a series of zigzags. The path is eroded in a couple of places but is a great help in this steep terrain, gaining the ridge just short of the summit. The view from here, looking down over Coire an Lochain to the scree-girt cone of Sgùrr Eilde Mòr, is a classic. After a bealach the route climbs to a minor top at a junction of ridges, then a wonderful section of ridge, alternating between grass and rocks underfoot, leads out to the airy summit of Binnein Mòr. One of the most elegant of the Munros, it's a fitting culmination for the whole Mamores range.

Back on the main spine of the Mamores ridge, another fine traverse leads over to the second Munro of the day, Na Gruagaichean ('the maidens'). A sharp drop in the ridge divides this summit from its slightly lower sister peak, with the huge bulk of Ben Nevis as the backdrop. For the descent, follow the south ridge out to Leachd na h-Aire. There are great views down the Kinlochleven but the descent from here is rough going, pathless and very steep at times. Eventually a track is reached with some relief, and paths lead down through the woods to return to the start, with a brief detour to see the impressive Grey Mares Tail Waterfall.

BINNEIN MÒR & NA GRUAGAICHEAN
DISTANCE: 13.6KM/8.4MILES » **TOTAL ASCENT:** 1,236M/4,055FT » **START GR:** NN 188622 » **TIME:** ALLOW 8 HOURS **SATNAV:** PH50 4QT » **MAP:** OS EXPLORER 392, BEN NEVIS & FORT WILLIAM, 1:25,000 » **REFRESHMENTS:** MO'S OR THE BOTHY BAR, KINLOCHLEVEN » **NAVIGATION:** GOOD MAP READING SKILLS AND MOUNTAIN EXPERIENCE REQUIRED.

Directions – Binnein Mòr & Na Gruagaichean

5 The walk starts from the Grey Mares Tail car park next to St Paul's church at the back of the northern part of Kinlochleven, known as Kinlochmore. **Take the path into the woods,** signed for *Spean Bridge*. Very soon **turn left** at a T-junction of paths and then **fork right** on to a path with steps. Climb through the trees, ignoring smaller paths off. At a junction **fork left** to cross the stream. The route now climbs through the woods; the original zigzag path has been eroded by shortcuts, it's best to **stick to the old route** to avoid worsening the damage. Eventually the trees are left behind and the now clear path leads across moorland.

2 **Fork left** just before reaching a vehicle track and soon **cross the track to follow an old stalkers' path opposite**. Cross a stream and start climbing the flank of Sgòr Eilde Beag. **Keep left** on the zigzagging path, avoiding a faint muddy path straight ahead that leads nowhere. At the top of the zigzags, traverse the slope on the path and then **bear left at a fork**, soon joining another stalkers' path which crosses an area of loose ground before continuing up to the ridge. Follow the straightforward grassy slope to the summit of Sgòr Eilde Beag and enjoy the stunning views.

SGÙRR EILDE MÒR ACROSS COIRE AN LOCHAIN

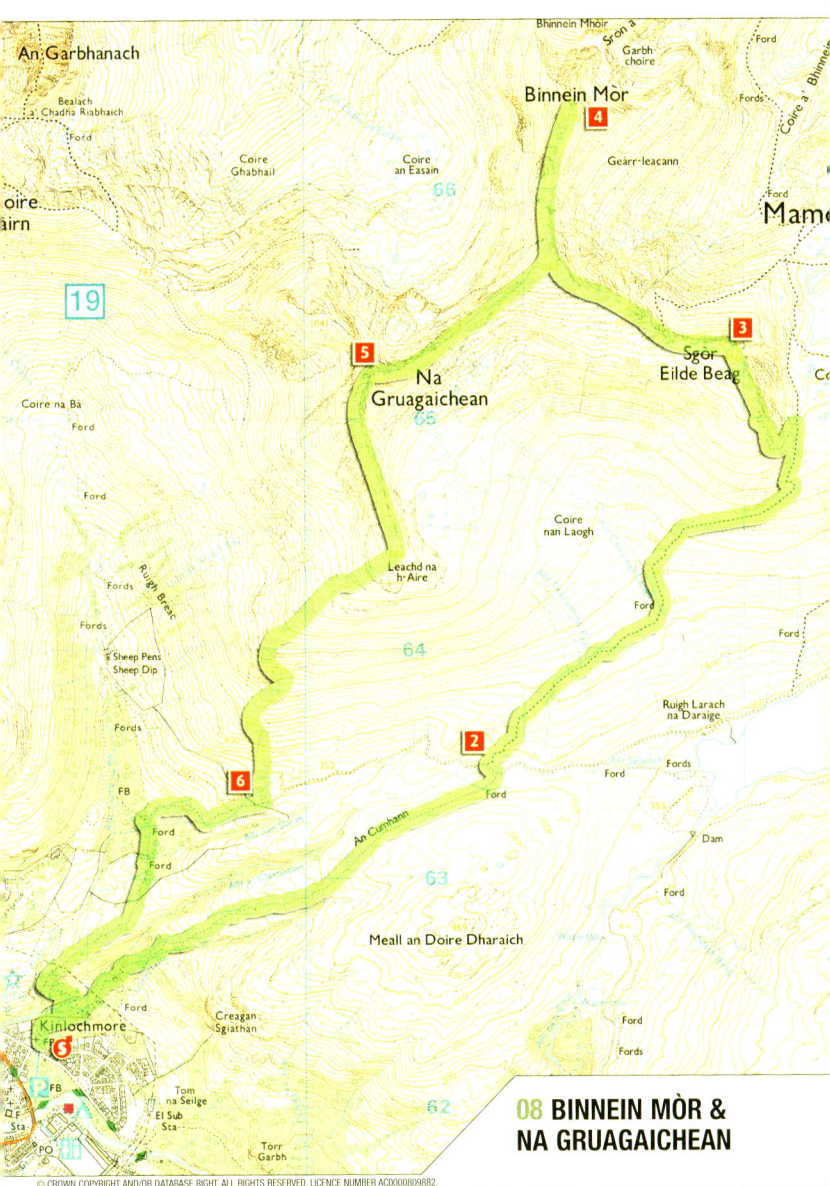

Directions – Binnein Mòr & Na Gruagaichean continued...

3 **Follow the broad ridge**, crossing a bealach where another path comes up from the right. Head uphill on the ridge to a minor peak at 1,062m. **Take the ridge heading north,** a detour along an excellent section of ridge, to reach the summit of Binnein Mòr.

4 The highest Munro in the Mamores, this is a fabulous and airy viewpoint. Turn around to **retrace the ridge route** back to the 1,062m peak. Now **aim south-west along a narrowing ridge,** crossing grassy turf and then broken stones to reach the bealach. From here it's a straightforward but very rocky climb to the summit of Na Gruagaichean at 1,056m, the second Munro of the day.

5 From here the sweeping ridge to the north-west provides a fabulous foreground to looming Ben Nevis behind. This route **takes the south ridge,** follow it to Leachd na h-Aire at 880m which provides an aerial view over Kinlochleven and Loch Leven. **Descend west-south-west** from the cairn following traces of paths at first. **Aim south-west down steep ground**, crossing a small boulder field. **Continue the descent,** bearing west-south-west on the now pathless and tiring ground. As the track below comes into view at last **aim south to meet it** where it passes through the deer fence.

6 **Turn left** on to the track and soon **bear right** on a path downhill. Go through the gate in the fence and continue ahead, eventually heading down through the woods. At a footbridge **turn left** (you can detour right here to visit the waterfall) and climb up the other side to retrace the outward route for the final few steps back to the start.

APPROACHING NA GRUAGAICHEAN

BEN NEVIS FROM STOB BÀN

09 Stob Bàn & Mullach nan Coirean   12.7km/7.9miles

The sharp rocky peak of Stob Bàn is one of the finest in the Mamores; with its neighbour Mullach nan Coirean it makes a magnificent circuit from Glen Nevis.

Glen Nevis » Allt Coire a' Mhusgain » Stob Bàn » Mullach nan Coirean » Riabhach Ridge » Glen Nevis

Start
Lower Falls car park (parking charge), Glen Nevis GR: NN 145683.

The Walk

The westernmost two Munros on the ridge forming the Mamores contrast starkly; Stob Bàn is a rocky, rugged and magnificent peak, while Mullach nan Coirean is an uncharacteristically rounded summit to terminate this fine range. The route begins by the Polldubh Falls in Glen Nevis, and takes an old stalkers' path that leads towards Coire a' Mhusgain. This stretch is a delight, with scattered deciduous trees clinging above a deep ravine where the Allt Coire a' Mhusgain tumbles on its way to join the River Nevis. A series of zigzags aids the climb to the upper corrie, and the path then traverses the slope before another calf-screaming pull leads up to the main ridge of the Mamores.

From this first vantage point Stob Bàn looks magnificent. The mountain's name means 'white peak', a reference to the shattered quartzite that litters the summit. The ridge leading up to it begins on grass but soon narrows and steepens, curving round above the dramatic north-east face on a rocky climb to reach the top. The huge cairn is an excellent place to hunker down and drink in the view, given real drama and depth with the ground falling away at your feet almost to the floor of Glen Nevis, with the great bulk of the Ben beyond.

The initial descent is over loose rocks, but soon a path is reached. A long and undulating grassy ridge includes one narrow and rocky (but straightforward) section of crest before reaching the second Munro of the round, Mullach nan Coirean. From here the descent is long but the views are great most of the way; you are likely to spot red deer. Eventually the forestry which clads the flanks of Glen Nevis is reached; the descent continues through the trees to reach the road and the start.

STOB BÀN & MULLACH NAN COIREAN

DISTANCE: 12.7KM/7.9MILES » **TOTAL ASCENT:** 1,157M/3,796FT » **START** GR: NN 145683 » **TIME:** ALLOW 7 HOURS **SATNAV:** PH33 6SY » **MAP:** OS EXPLORER 392, BEN NEVIS & FORT WILLIAM, 1:25,000 » **REFRESHMENTS:** GLEN NEVIS RESTAURANT & BAR » **NAVIGATION:** GOOD NAVIGATION SKILLS NEEDED.

APPROACHING STOB BÀN

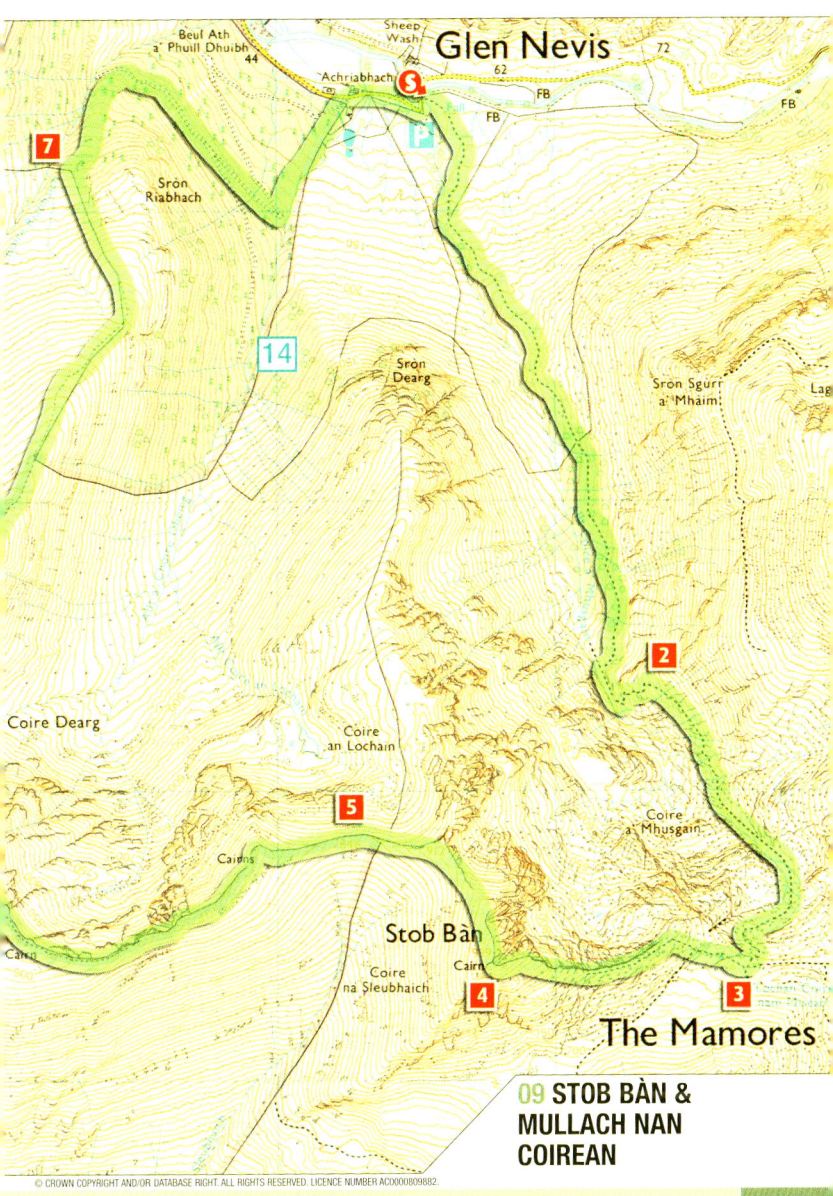

09 **STOB BÀN & MULLACH NAN COIREAN**

Directions – Stob Bàn & Mullach nan Coirean

S The Lower Falls car park is three quarters of the way along Glen Nevis, just before the bridge at Polldubh Falls. **Walk down towards the bridge** but before you get to it **turn right through a gate** on to a track; don't confuse this with the footpath a wee bit further on which heads up beside the River Nevis. The track soon narrows to a path and follows the east side of the Allt Coire a' Mhusgain. As the path starts to climb it can be boggy. **Keep heading uphill, now on an old stalkers' path** and becoming drier underfoot. Go through a gate and follow the path, which keeps well above the steep ravine with the Allt Coire a' Mhusagain. **Head through some scattered woodland** and pass below a crag before heading up a series of zigzags.

2 At the top of these the path contours the slope before eventually **climbing more zigzags** next to a waterfall. Stay on the path to cross the upper corrie and **climb up to the shoulder on the ridge**. There are great views back down to Glen Nevis.

3 **Bear west along the ridge,** aiming for the prominent peak of Stob Bàn. As the ridge narrows and climbs the grass gives way to the broken quartzite rocks which give Stob Bàn its name. **On the steep final approach to the summit keep left** before reaching the summit.

4 From here there is a fantastic view of Ben Nevis, and to the east the massive peak of Sgùrr a' Mhàim dominates the view, which is connected to the main spine of the Mamores by the airy Devil's Ridge. **Bear north to descend** from the summit, crossing broken stony ground at first. **Cross a rocky knoll** and soon the going gets easier underfoot, picking up a grassy path. Bear left to bypass the next hillock if you want, **aiming west to reach the bealach** at 846m.

5 The fine ridgewalking continues, climbing at first to a minor summit among quartzite. **Keep on the ridge**; when it narrows to a rocky crest you can use a bypass on the left if need be. The ridge then broadens and climbs to a broad plateau at 917m. **Descend for a short distance and then climb** to the huge cairn marking the summit of Mullach nan Coirean at 939m.

6 From here the outlook over Loch Linnhe is sensational. From the summit **head north along the ridge** which **soon curves to head east-north-east**. Eventually a fence and stile are reached. **Don't cross the stile but continue down the left-hand side of the fence**. Ignore a second stile and stay on the left-hand side of the fence, crossing increasingly boggy and steep ground.

7 As the bottom of the slope and the Allt a' Choire Riabhaich is approached, **cross a stile and follow the path** which is now much drier underfoot. Pass through some birchwoods and an old felled plantation to reach a forestry track. **Turn right** along the track and at a junction **branch left** heading downhill. **At a sharp bend turn right on to a path** to descend through the trees on a direct route back to Achriabhach. At the road **turn right** to reach the car park.

THE HEAD OF GLEN NEVIS

STEALL MEADOWS FROM THE LOWER SLOPES

10 An Steall & An Gearanach 8.7km/5.4miles

Pass through the dramatic Nevis Gorge to reach the impressive An Steall waterfall before a very steep ascent leads to the summit of this fine Munro.

Glen Nevis » Nevis Gorge » An Steall » Allt Coire Chadha Chaoruinn » An Gearanach » Allt Coire Chadha Chaoruinn » An Steall » Nevis Gorge » Glen Nevis

Start
Car park at the end of the Glen Nevis road. GR: NN 167691.

The Walk
The Nevis Gorge was described by the mountaineer and writer W.H. Murray as being of 'Himalayan character' and 'one of the scenic wonders of Scotland'. The dramatic path through this tree-clad gorge to reach the magnificent An Steall waterfall and its wire suspension bridge is a classic short walk in itself. The land here is owned by a conservation charity, the John Muir Trust, who have done a lot of work in recent years repairing the rocky path and encouraging growth of the native woodland.

You can test your balance and fear of heights with a crossing of the infamous wire bridge, or take the coward's option of a wade across the water just above the bridge – unless the river is in spate. A boggy path leads to the base of the waterfall and another potentially problematic river crossing. There's a further section of very wet ground to cross before a stalkers' path finally heads uphill and the going underfoot improves.

A steep, long climb eventually leads to the ridge and an airy walk to An Gearanach's summit; this Munro provides a backdrop to the waterfall. From here the peaks making up the great horseshoe known as the Ring of Steall can be seen; a full round of them makes for a long mountain day with a great deal of scrambling – a classic challenge best left for the fittest and most experienced hillwalkers.

For the route described here, though, one Munro is enough. Turn back at An Gearanach and retrace your steps back down into Glen Nevis to enjoy the Nevis Gorge again on your way back.

AN STEALL & AN GEARANACH
DISTANCE: 8.7KM/5.4MILES » **TOTAL ASCENT:** 963M/3,159FT » **START GR:** NN 167691 » **TIME:** ALLOW 5.5 HOURS
SATNAV: PH33 6SY » **MAP:** OS EXPLORER 392, BEN NEVIS & FORT WILLIAM, 1:25,000 » **REFRESHMENTS:** GLEN NEVIS RESTAURANT & BAR » **NAVIGATION:** GOOD NAVIGATION SKILLS NEEDED.

Directions – An Steall & An Gearanach

5 There is a car park at the far end of the minor road up Glen Nevis. If using the summer bus from Fort William, it goes only as far as Polldubh Falls, leaving a couple of kilometres of road walking. **Take the path leading from the car park** into the woodland. After a short distance the path narrows, contouring the flanks of the Nevis Gorge. It's rocky and can be slippery when wet – the wooded slope on the right plunges steeply to the Water of Nevis tumbling far below. **Keep following the path** as it winds it way through the gorge, passing between some massive boulders at one point.

2 **Stay on the path** when it emerges from the trees and heads across open ground. Cross a flower-strewn meadow backed with a view of An Steall, a spectacular braided waterfall cascading down the high mountain slopes opposite. When the path forks just before a corner **turn right** to cross the grass, aiming for the wire bridge over the river.

3 **Cross the river.** The bridge consists of one wire for your feet and two for your hands and wobbles unnervingly high above the water – it serves as a right of passage for many hillwalkers. At times of low water it is usually possible to cross on stepping stones immediately upriver. In spate conditions both this and the next unbridged crossing at the foot of An Steall become impassable. Once over the water **turn left**, pass the private hut and **follow a rough and boggy path** through the trees towards An Steall. **Carefully cross the water** at the base of the waterfall and **continue ahead** over very wet and marshy ground, curving round the foot of the hill. Once around this corner **bear right** to pick up a stalkers' path leading uphill. As height is gained **continue up the path,** skirting around a couple of places where the original path has been destroyed by landslides. Beyond these the path improves, **continue climbing** and follow the path as it bears right to traverse the corrie. **Follow a series of zigzags steeply uphill** and then **aim right** to reach the shoulder of a grassy ridge.

4 **Bear left** to follow the path that climbs south-east up the ridge. After a steep climb there is a gentler section before a final climb to reach the summit of An Gearanach. At 982m this is a fine viewpoint with a great vista of Ben Nevis behind and the dramatic An Garbhanach ridge ahead.

5 Many walkers will continue along the ridge from here to complete the Ring of Steall horseshoe taking in four Munros and a number of lesser peaks. This makes for a strenuous day involving a good deal of scrambling over both An Garbhanach and on the Devil's Ridge to Sgùrr a' Mhàim. Don't attempt the round unless you are properly prepared and experienced, and note that the safe descent from Sgùrr a' Mhàim is down the north-west ridge – there is no exit from the valley of the Allt Coire a' Mhàil above An Steall.

After enjoying the summit views **turn around and retrace your steps** all the way back down to the floor of Glen Nevis. If water levels are low it is possible to avoid the boggy ground on the approach to An Steall (otherwise retrace the outward route via the falls and wire bridge) – **head straight across the grassy ground** to reach the Water of Nevis and **cross at a shallow point (dry conditions only)**. **Turn left** to follow the riverside path. **Keep straight on** at the junction where the left fork leads to the wire bridge. **Continue on the path** and follow it back down through the Nevis Gorge to the start.

10 AN STEALL & AN GEARANACH

SECTION 3

Fort William & the Great Glen

Set on the shores of Loch Linnhe, Fort William styles itself as the Outdoor Capital of the UK – a title it well deserves. Set at the end of Scotland's most popular long-distance path and at the foot of its highest mountain, the town is a magnet for walkers, climbers and adventurers.

Ben Nevis – or 'The Ben', as it is affectionately known – has some of the country's most magnificent crags in its stunning north face, while the sylvan delights of Glen Nevis wind for miles into the mountains. The Nevis Range continues eastwards over the great bulk of the Aonachs, Beag and Mòr, linking eastwards to the scree-girt and shapely Grey Corries – a fine backdrop to the famous view from the Commando Memorial at Spean Bridge.

BEN NEVIS FROM THE SHORE OF LOCH LINNHE

BEN NEVIS FROM THE CIC HUT

FORT WILLIAM FROM COW HILL

11 Cow Hill

11km/6.8miles

Lying between Fort William and Ben Nevis, the modest heights of Cow Hill offer fine mountain and loch views and can be tackled from the centre of town.

The Parade, Fort William » Leisure Centre » Glen Nevis Forestry Track » Fèith na Sgàthaiche » Cow Hill » Fèith na Sgàthaiche » Upper Auchintore » The Parade, Fort William

Start

North end of Fort William High Street (various parking options available in Fort William; mainly pay and display). GR: NN 104741.

The Walk

Visitors arriving in Fort William are often striving for a first view of Ben Nevis – but do so in vain. Cow Hill blocks the view of the Ben from the town, but provides a fantastic short day in its own right, without the need for any transport from Fort William. The walk starts from the High Street, passing the local leisure centre, whose excellent pool and steam room are perfect for soothing aching hillwalkers' limbs.

A waymarked path climbs briefly and then begins a traverse of the lower slopes. Soon the Sugar Loaf is reached, a viewpoint with a handy bench to enjoy the outlook over Loch Linnhe and along the Great Glen. It was from here in 1746 that the Jacobites, led by Bonnie Prince Charlie, fired on the troops stationed in Fort William, which was built as one of a chain of fortifications along the Great Glen. In Gaelic the town's name is An Gearasdan – 'the garrison'.

Soon the route curves round into Glen Nevis, with views across to Meall an t-Suidhe, and then to the mighty Ben itself. A steep track climbs to an area where peat was traditionally cut and dried to be used as fuel to heat homes. While peat has largely been replaced by modern heating locally, it is still cut in some parts of Scotland, especially the Hebrides, though the days when whole communities would cut peat together are long gone.

A meandering path detours up to the summit of Cow Hill, crowned by a transmitter mast but also a spectacular view over the town and mountains beyond – a vista to whet any hillwalker's appetite. The descent route follows a path and then a track with views down Loch Linnhe and out to the sea and islands. The outskirts of Fort William are reached and the route returns along the pedestrianised High Street.

COW HILL

DISTANCE: 11KM/6.8MILES » **TOTAL ASCENT:** 426M/1,398FT » **START GR:** NN 104741 » **TIME:** ALLOW 4 HOURS
SATNAV: PH33 6AZ » **MAP:** OS EXPLORER 392, BEN NEVIS & FORT WILLIAM, 1:25,000 » **REFRESHMENTS:** THE WILDCAT OR BLACK ISLE BAR, FORT WILLIAM » **NAVIGATION:** CLEAR, WAYMARKED PATHS.

Directions – Cow Hill

1 Begin from the grassy park known as The Parade at the north end of the High Street. With the Alexandra Hotel on your right, **cross the park** to the main A82 road and **turn right** along the pavement. Continue until the leisure centre and **turn right** along the far side of the building, passing through a car park to reach an information board at the start of a path heading uphill into the woods. **Climb the path ahead** which zigzags uphill. **Keep left,** ignoring smaller paths off to the right.

2 When another path is reached **turn left** to traverse around the slopes of the hill. A short way further on, ignore the path to the right and **stay on the route** signed for the *Braveheart car park*. A small summit with a bench is reached. Known as the Sugar Loaf, it's a great vantage point over Fort William. Keep following signs for the *Braveheart car park*, ignoring another path which branches to the right. **Keep straight ahead** as the path heads through young birch, willow and alder trees. Pass the Braveheart car park seen to the left of the path and **keep right** at a forestry track, signed *Cow Hill summit via the peat track*. The track heads through the forestry plantation for 1km to a signed junction.

3 **Turn right** here, following the sign for *Cow Hill*. **Climb steeply** with ever improving views across Glen Nevis to Ben Nevis behind. Go through a gate to leave the trees and **follow a track** across open moorland at a more gentle gradient. Soon there are views to Loch Linnhe ahead. Continue until you reach a junction with a larger track.

4 **Turn right** signed for *Cow Hill*. Pass a gate and descend briefly before the final climb to the summit of Cow Hill. The summit has a fenced mast, pass round this for the best views beyond.

5 The view over Loch Linnhe – with Fort William, Caol and Corpach – fills the foreground, with Loch Eil and seemingly endless ranges of mountains beyond. **Return to the track** junction where you turned off for Cow Hill and continue straight ahead. **Head downhill** with good views of Loch Linnhe ahead. After a bench the track bends right, **stay on it** to reach a gate at the road.

6 **Turn right** along the road which leads downhill to the edge of Fort William. After passing the school on the left watch out for a path signed *Town Centre via Achintore Gardens*. **Turn left** along this path and, after a set of steps, keep straight ahead down the road to reach the main road. Cross this and **turn right** to follow a path along the side of Loch Linnhe. At the roundabout use the crossings to **take the middle road** ahead, which is the south end of the High Street, and return to the start.

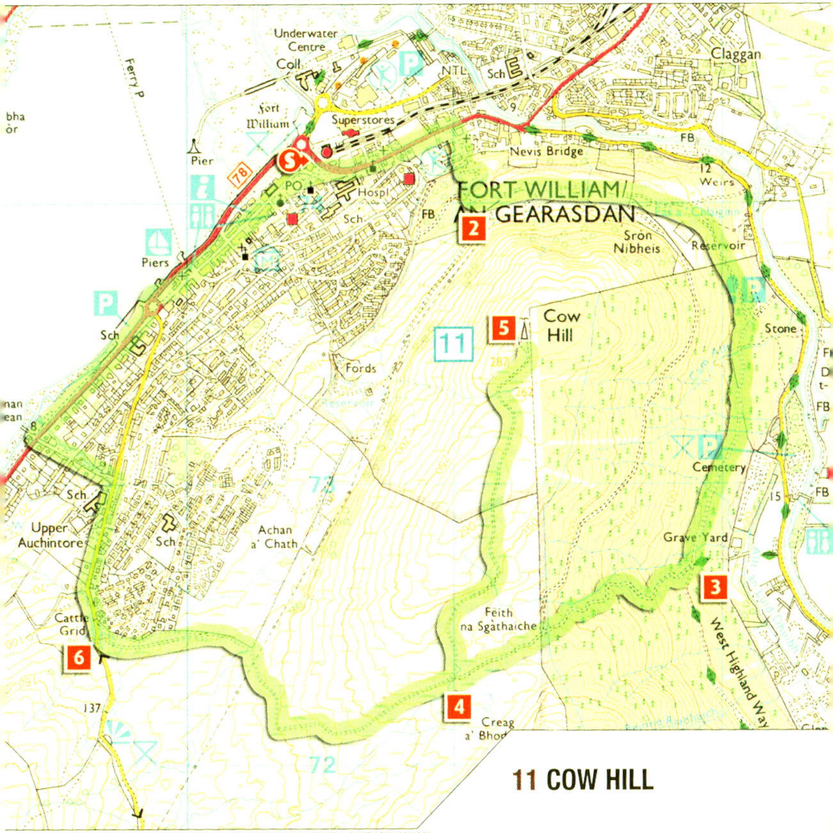

11 COW HILL

APPROACHING THE NORTH FACE

12 Ben Nevis North Face 11.4km/7.1miles

The true majesty of Ben Nevis is revealed on this excursion beneath the mighty cliffs of its spectacular north face.

Torlundy » Forest » Allt a' Mhuilinn » CIC hut » Allt a' Mhuilinn » Forest » Torlundy

Start
North Face car park, Torlundy, off the A82 north-east of Fort William. GR: NN 145764.

The Walk
The north face of Ben Nevis remains unseen by most visitors, whether they are ascending to the summit via the Mountain Track, or admiring its rounded flanks from near Fort William. Yet it is here that Britain's highest mountain reveals its alpine character, with a myriad of great rocky buttresses, ridges and gullies. A Mecca for both rock and ice climbers, the north face may be out of the league of many walkers, but this walk to see it close up gives a dramatic insight into this vertical world.

Heading up from a car park near Torlundy, the route climbs up through mixed woodland and forestry before emerging to the first views of the Ben itself. The route continues upstream alongside the Allt a' Mhuilinn. There are a few lovely small pools, great for cooling off on the way back on a hot summer's day.

As the looming wall of the north face is approached the path crosses the burn and reaches the CIC Hut. Erected in the late 1920s by the parents of Charles Inglis Clark, who was killed in action during World War I, this club hut has been used as a base by many of the climbing legends who have put up new routes on the Ben, including Tom Patey, Dougal Haston, Don Whillans, Joe Brown, Jimmy Marshall and, more recently, Dave MacLeod. The hut is not open to the public, so respect the privacy of those staying there; for ordinary pedestrians, the attraction is the setting, overwhelming in its scale and majesty. Binoculars are a great help in spotting climbers and mountaineers heading up the towering buttresses and ridges that soar above.

The return to Torlundy is by retracing your steps, with good views over Loch Linnhe and Loch Eil before the last leg through the trees.

BEN NEVIS NORTH FACE
DISTANCE: 11.4KM/7.1MILES » **TOTAL ASCENT:** 651M/2,136FT » **START GR:** NN 145764 » **TIME:** ALLOW 3.5 HOURS
SATNAV: PH33 6SW » **MAP:** OS EXPLORER 392, BEN NEVIS & FORT WILLIAM, 1:25,000 » **REFRESHMENTS:** THE WILDCAT, FORT WILLIAM, OR JJ'S CAFE, LOCHYBRIDGE » **NAVIGATION:** STRAIGHTFORWARD.

Directions – Ben Nevis North Face

S The Forestry and Land Scotland North Face car park is signed from the A82 a few kilometres north-east of Fort William, accessed via a track from Torlundy. To begin the walk, **take the track** past the vehicle barrier and, when the track curves left, **turn right** on to a path, signed *North Face Trail*. **Go straight ahead** at a junction with the Puggy Line Trail, then **keep right** on the main path at a fork. The path now winds uphill. Continue ahead when a smaller path joins from the left. Soon a bench is passed with views over the head of Loch Linnhe and along Loch Eil. At the next junction **keep right**, signed for the *North Face and CIC Hut*. Pass a picnic table with another superb view. When a track is reached, with a bridge on the right, **go straight ahead** up the track, soon passing a hydro dam. At a track junction **turn right**, now with stunning views of Ben Nevis ahead. At the top of the forestry the track ends.

2 **Cross the stile** to head up the well-made path which works its way up the east side of the Allt a' Mhuilinn. The views to the looming north face of Ben Nevis become more impressive with each step.

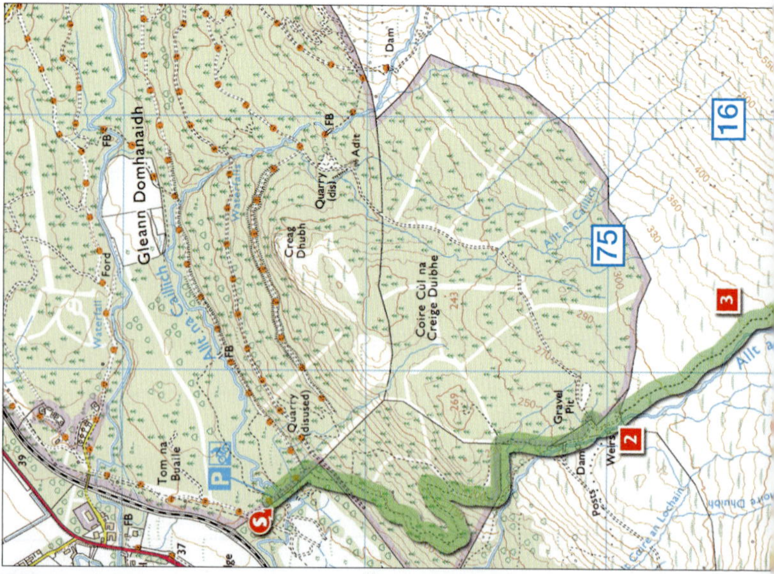

3 **Ignore the smaller path which branches left** (this eventually leads to Càrn Mòr Dearg and its spectacular arête which provides an exhilarating link to Ben Nevis – see route 15b). **Continue up the path** keeping an eye out for scramblers and climbers on the huge buttresses and gullies which divide the giant cliffs. The path moves further away from the water before returning towards it.

4 **Cross the water** at a small ford (may be a problem in spate) and head towards the Charles Inglis Clark Memorial Hut. Used as a private hut for mountaineers, it is not accessible to the public, so please respect the privacy of its occupants. The hut is right at the foot of Tower Ridge, a classic mountaineering route up the Ben in both summer and winter. From here you must retrace your steps all the way back to the start.

12 BEN NEVIS NORTH FACE

BEN NEVIS FROM INVERSKILAVULIN

13 Beinn Bhàn

8.3km/5.2miles

Rising between Glen Loy and Loch Arkaig, the Corbett of Beinn Bhàn is a neglected hill with steep flanks guarding its spacious, plateau-like summit and excellent views.

Inverskilavulin Bridge » above the Allt Coire Mhuilinn » Cairn above Coire Mhuilinn » Beinn Bhàn » Inverskilavulin Bridge

Start

Small parking area next to Inverskilavulin Bridge in Glen Loy. GR: NN 125831.

The Walk

Few people venture off the Great Glen into Glen Loy, its narrow strip of tarmac running through conifer plantations mixed with relics of the ancient Atlantic oak wood which once clothed much of Scotland's West Highland coast. The ascent of Beinn Bhàn gives a fairly short hillwalk by Lochaber standards, rewarded with superb views of Ben Nevis and its neighbours across the Great Glen, as well as aerial vistas of Loch Arkaig.

Starting from a small parking area near Inverskilavulin Bridge a few miles up the glen, the route begins along a track before fairly quickly reaching the open hillside. Underfoot the going can be boggy as a rough path skirts the woodland lining the Allt Coire Mhuilinn. The ascent steepens and the path peters out as the open slopes are tackled. A relentless climb is rewarded by increasingly dramatic views back towards the north face of Ben Nevis.

Eventually the gradient begins to ease as the route heads up a broad ridge, and then the rim of Coire Mhuilinn is reached; there is a cairn at the start of the plateau. From here there's a great panorama of Loch Arkaig and the mountains beyond. In good weather the walk around the top of Coire Mhuilinn is a delight; if you are less lucky, a line of fence posts may be a useful aid to navigation. These lead to the cairn and trig point that mark the summit of Beinn Bhàn, a great place to linger and enjoy the solitude and silence.

The descent is fairly straightforward, eventually picking up traces of a path and crossing some stony ground to emerge near the houses at Inverskilavulin, from where the outward track is followed back to the start.

BEINN BHÀN

DISTANCE: 8.3KM/5.2MILES » **TOTAL ASCENT:** 776M/2,546FT » **START GR:** NN 125831 » **TIME:** ALLOW 4.5 HOURS
SATNAV: PH33 7PB » **MAP:** OS EXPLORER 399, LOCH ARKAIG, 1:25,000 » **REFRESHMENTS:** THE BRIDGE CAFE, SPEAN BRIDGE
NAVIGATION: STRAIGHTFORWARD IN GOOD WEATHER; GOOD NAVIGATION SKILLS NEEDED IN POOR VISIBILITY.

Directions – Beinn Bhàn

❺▶ There is limited parking on a forestry track to the left just before Inverskilavulin Bridge; take care not to block any gates or obstruct the track. **Cross the bridge** and **turn right** towards Inverskilavulin. When a gate is reached **turn left,** following a faint grassy track uphill, **keeping to the left** of the fence. Underfoot the going can be wet in places.

2 **Don't cross the bridge** to the right, instead **keep just left of the trees**. This woodland on the banks of the Allt Coire Mhuilinn is an important habitat for several species of rare butterflies. The path continues climbing, passing through patches of bracken in high summer, and keeping parallel with the burn on the right. At the end of the trees **bear slightly left** and continue uphill on the broad ridge of increasingly steep ground. Eventually the gradient eases a little before a **final steep climb** up to the plateau above Coire Mhuilinn.

3 A cairn marks the start of the almost flat walk around the rim of the coire. **Follow the line of old fence posts**, particularly useful in poor visibility. **Reach the low point** at the back of the coire and **climb up the far side** before aiming **east-south-east** to reach the mountain summit.

4 Marked by a trig point and cairn, Beinn Bhàn is an excellent vantage point with great views to the north face of Ben Nevis, numerous smaller mountain summits and the waters of Loch Arkaig and Loch Lochy. Leave the summit by aiming **south-west**. Stay on the least steep ground, soon turning south, with the view of Ben Nevis directly ahead; there is an intermittent path in places. After descending for 500m start to **slowly curve to the right** to descend the easiest ground above the Allt Coire Mhuilinn. When the fence below comes into sight **aim to the right** to the point where the fence nears the burn.

5 **Pick up a path** heading over a small ridge and round the corner of the fence, and keep between the burn and the fence. Just before the fence forming the boundary for the houses at Inverskilavulin **turn right** to reach a wooden footbridge. **Cross the bridge** and **turn left,** retracing the outward route back to the start.

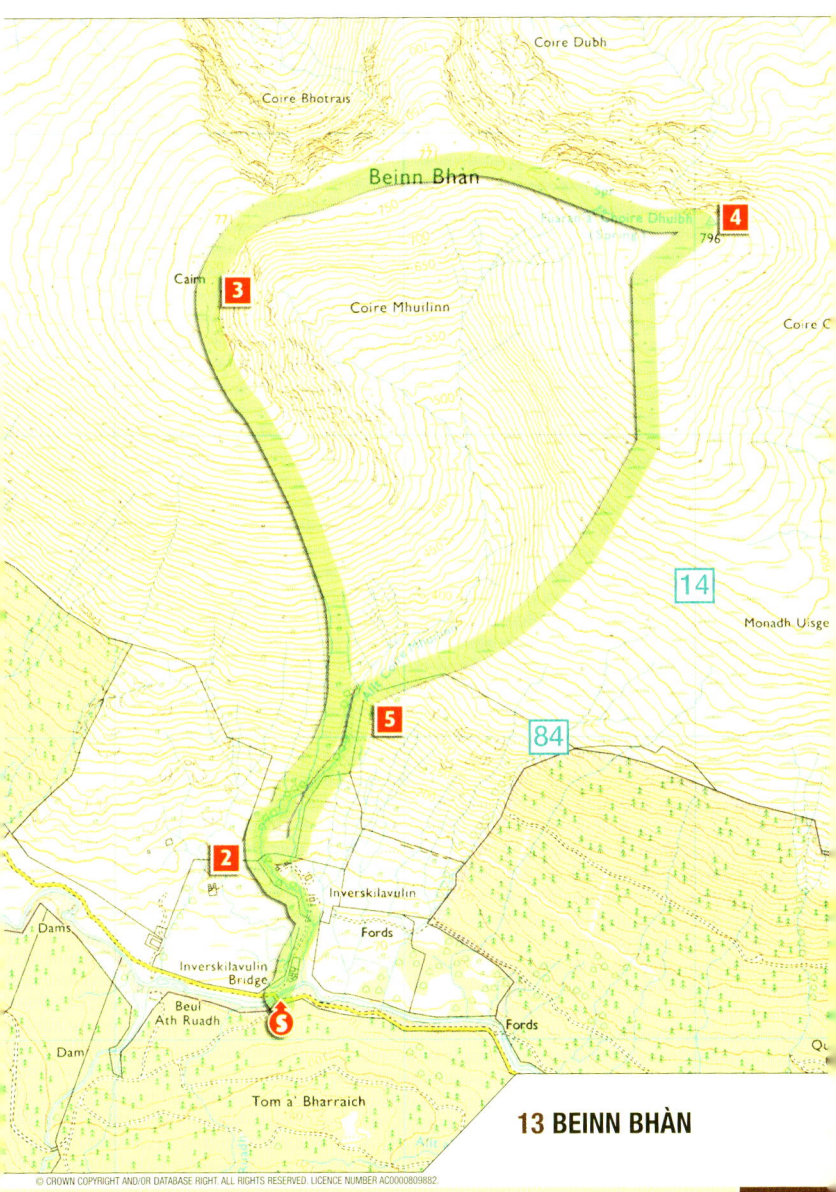

13 BEINN BHÀN

VIEW FROM AN T-SOCACH

14 Sgùrr na h-Eanchainne & Druim na Sgrìodain

13.2km/8.2miles

Take the ferry over the Corran Narrows to tackle this very steep and rugged mountain circuit, offering solitude and spectacular views.

Corran Ferry » Cille Mhaodain » Sgùrr na h-Eanchainne » Druim na Sgrìodain » An t-Socach » Allt a' Choire Dhuibh » Mast » Corran Ferry

Start
Corran Ferry slipway, Corran. GR: NN 016637.

The Walk
The great peak of Sgùrr na h-Eanchainne dominates the view across the Corran Narrows on Loch Linnhe – it is much admired but seldom climbed. This short, mostly pathless, mountain circuit is surprisingly tough. To reach it, the Corran Ferry takes just over five minutes to negotiate the swirling waters across the narrows.

On the far side the route heads first for the ancestral burial ground of the local Clan MacLean, who have owned the land since the 1430s, having grabbed it during a raid on the occupying Clan MacMaster. The MacMaster chief fled for the ferry, shouting for the boatman to aid his escape, but he was out fishing and refused. The MacLean chief, hearing that the boatman had proved disloyal to his own chief, hung him from his oars. Folklore states that MacLeans will remain on this land until the waterfalls known as MacLean's Towel dry up. The level of rainfall in this part of Scotland suggests that the clan is pretty safe.

The route climbs very steeply up pathless terrain to gain the ridge of Sgùrr na h-Eanchainne. Soon the small summit is reached – an amazing viewpoint. Ben Nevis dominates, while the peaks of Glen Coe look magnificent, and the outlook down Loch Linnhe and out to sea is spectacular.

Rough and wet ground leads to the highest summit of the day, 1.5 kilometres further on. At 734 metres Druim na Sgrìodain is a Graham. The Grahams are often the next target for keen hillbaggers who have completed the Munros and Corbetts.

The descent is rough and steep, with dangerous terrain – careful navigation is essential. The waterfalls can be spectacular after heavy rain. Eventually flatter ground is reached with some relief, and tracks lead back to Corran; if calling at the pub, make sure you don't miss the last evening ferry!

SGÙRR NA H-EANCHAINNE & DRUIM NA SGRÌODAIN

DISTANCE: 13.2KM/8.2MILES » **TOTAL ASCENT:** 843M/2,766FT » **START GR:** NN 016637 » **TIME:** ALLOW 6.5 HOURS
SATNAV: PH33 7BF » **MAP:** OS EXPLORER 391, ARDGOUR & STRONTIAN, 1:25,000 » **REFRESHMENTS:** THE INN AT ARDGOUR, CORRAN » **NAVIGATION:** EXCELLENT MAP READING SKILLS ESSENTIAL, PARTICULARLY ON DESCENT.

BEN NEVIS FROM SGÙRR NA H-EANCHAINNE

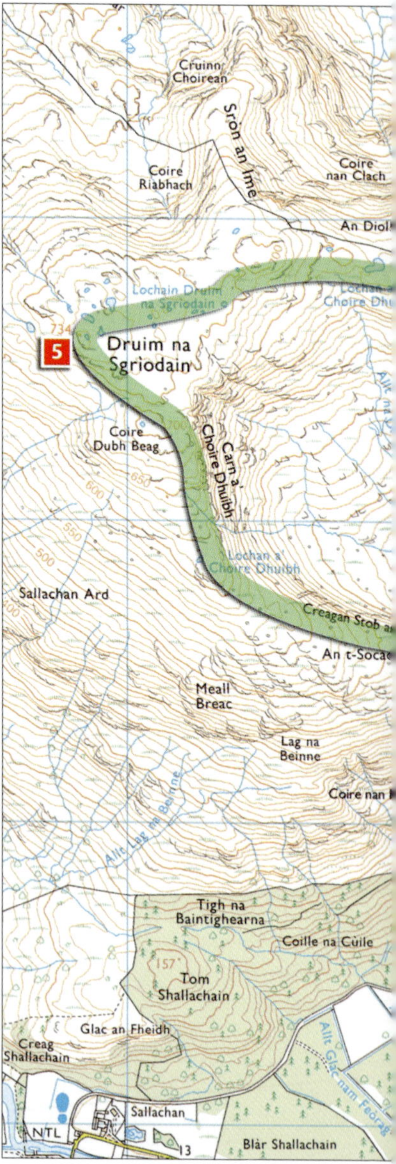

DAY WALKS IN FORT WILLIAM & GLEN COE

14 SGÙRR NA H-EANCHAINNE & DRUIM NA SGRÌODAIN

Directions — Sgùrr na h-Eanchainne & Druim na Sgrìodain

1 The Corran Ferry carries passengers and vehicles across the narrows of Loch Linnhe, 14km south-west of Fort William. Running every twenty minutes at peak times and then every half an hour, disruption is rare but it's best to check the website. The Fort William side is referred to as Nether Lochaber. There is parking and toilets here, so you can leave your car and head across on foot. If starting on the Ardgour side there is parking opposite Ardgour Parish Church. Once off the ferry **turn right** along the road, soon passing the Inn at Ardgour and continuing for a couple of kilometres.

2 At the far end of Camas na Cille **go through a gate** on the left into a field where a stone wall encloses the ancient graveyard of Cille Mhaodain – the ancestral burial ground of the MacLeans of Ardgour. **Pass to the right** of the graveyard and go through a gate in a stone wall. **Head left** to reach another gate which leads to the open hill. **Climb steeply** on an indistinct path, eventually heading up pathless ground with patches of bracken. Any breaks from the ascent are rewarded by the fabulous views opening up behind you to Loch Linnhe and Ben Nevis beyond. Once on a grassy hillock **keep heading west-north-west** (half right diagonally uphill) to reach the north ridge of Sgùrr na h-Eanchainne.

3 **Bear left to follow a line of fence posts,** heading south to arrive at the trig point marking the 731m top.

4 Although not the highest point on the route, this is the most prominent peak as seen from across Loch Linnhe, and it's the best viewpoint of the day with a grand panorama of peaks laid out from Glen Coe to Ben Nevis. Looking west, numerous islands dot the distant seascape. From the trig point **descend the broad west ridge**. The ground is mainly pathless and undulates over peat hags, passing a number of watery lochans. From the final lochan climb to the small cairn at the summit of Druim na Sgrìodain. This is the highest summit at 734m, but it lacks the drama of Sgùrr na h-Eanchainne.

5 From the summit **descend south-east,** soon following the ridge and skirting above the cliffs of Carn a' Choire Dhuibh. **Stay on the rough ridge** to reach the prow of An t-Socach, marked by a small cairn. **Aim east** from here at first, following a faint path down the steep, grassy ridge. Careful map reading is needed from now on as the direct route down is impassable due to crags. **Head east-north-east and cross the Allt a' Choire Dhuibh** above a series of waterfalls.

6 **Descend the very steep slopes** on the far side, keeping away from the burn and aiming for a telecommunications mast below. The ground is slippery and rocky in places so great care is needed to take a safe line. At the bottom **go through a gap in the fence and keep right** to pass the mast and take a muddy path through trees. **Branch left** at a fork; soon a track is reached, **turn right**. At the next junction **turn right** and cross a small stream before you **turn left** on to a surfaced lane leading to Clovullin village. **Take the next left** and follow a track past two lochans. At the road near the church **turn right** to return to the ferry.

SGÙRR NA H-EANCHAINNE FROM CORRAN

THE UPPER PART OF THE MOUNTAIN TRACK

15a Ben Nevis by the Mountain Track 15.8km/9.8miles

Britain's highest mountain is made tougher by the ascent beginning from near sea level. On a fine day the views are as extensive as you'd expect; the sense of achievement balanced by aching knees.

Glen Nevis » Creagan nan Gabhar » Path Junction near Lochan Meall an t-Suidhe » Red Burn » Ben Nevis » Red Burn » Path Junction near Lochan Meall an t-Suidhe » Creagan nan Gabhar » Glen Nevis

Start
Glen Nevis Visitor Centre car park (parking charge). GR: NN 122730.

The Walk

Britain's highest mountain, known affectionately as 'The Ben', stands at 1,345 metres (4,413 feet). The ascent is strenuous and long, but rewards with a real sense of achievement and camaraderie with fellow hikers. However the mountain is also a dangerous place; in poor weather the route needs expert navigation skills and proper equipment. As with all mountains, an ice axe and crampons are needed when there is snow; the snow often lasts into early summer.

The walk starts from Glen Nevis Visitor Centre where up-to-date information about conditions on the mountain can be obtained. After crossing the River Nevis the path soon starts to climb, with great views up the glen to the Mamores. The path was constructed in 1883 to serve the summit meteorological observatory that recorded the weather until 1904. Incredibly harsh conditions were endured by the early weathermen, who frequently had to dig through up to four feet of snow to get out of their summit shelter, and rope up to check their instruments safely.

It is unlikely you will be alone as over 100,000 people attempt to climb the Ben every year. The first recorded ascent was undertaken by Edinburgh botanist James Robertson in 1771, who was collecting plant species.

The route levels off near Lochan Meall an t-Suidhe. Beyond, it crosses the Red Burn and becomes a relentless climb on rocky, scree-covered ground. Careful navigation is required towards the summit due to the proximity of cliffs, especially on the descent. Many hillwalkers, avoiding the cliffs of the north face, have veered instead into Five Finger Gully; it's a notorious accident blackspot.

BEN NEVIS BY THE MOUNTAIN TRACK

DISTANCE: 15.8KM/9.8MILES » **TOTAL ASCENT:** 1,369M/4,491FT » **START GR:** NN 122730 » **TIME:** ALLOW 9 HOURS **SATNAV:** PH33 6PF » **MAP:** OS EXPLORER 392, BEN NEVIS & FORT WILLIAM, 1:25,000 » **REFRESHMENTS:** GLEN NEVIS RESTAURANT & BAR » **NAVIGATION:** GOOD MAP AND COMPASS SKILLS NEEDED ESPECIALLY ON DESCENT IN POOR WEATHER; BE PREPARED FOR VERY DIFFERENT CONDITIONS AT THE SUMMIT.

Directions – Ben Nevis by the Mountain Track

5 Take a moment to read the information and current weather/snow forecast in the Glen Nevis Visitor Centre before you set off. Although very popular, the ascent of Ben Nevis is strenuous and it cannot be overstated how different the weather is likely to be at the top. From the visitor centre **cross the bridge** over the River Nevis and **turn right**. Follow the riverbank for a short distance and **turn left** at a signed junction to walk between a wall and a fence.

2 **Climb the stile** and **cross the track** to meet the path that begins from the Ben Nevis Inn. **Turn right** and follow the path as it climbs across the hillside. The path passes above a small conifer plantation and meets the path coming up from the Glen Nevis Youth Hostel. **Continue straight ahead,** eventually following the path's wide zigzags as it continues to gain height. There are good views along Glen Nevis to the Mamores mountain range. **Cross two footbridges** and stay on the path as it climbs steeply, curving above the Allt na h-Urchaire or Red Burn.

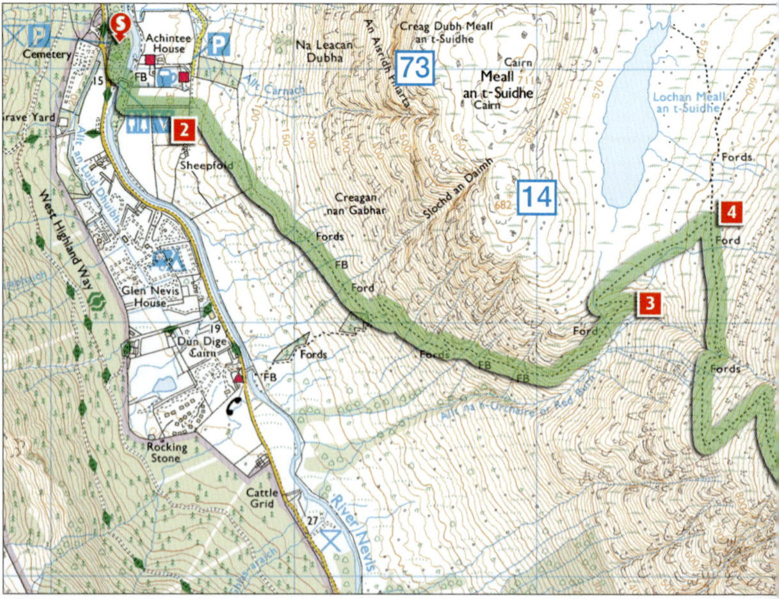

84 DAY WALKS IN FORT WILLIAM & GLEN COE

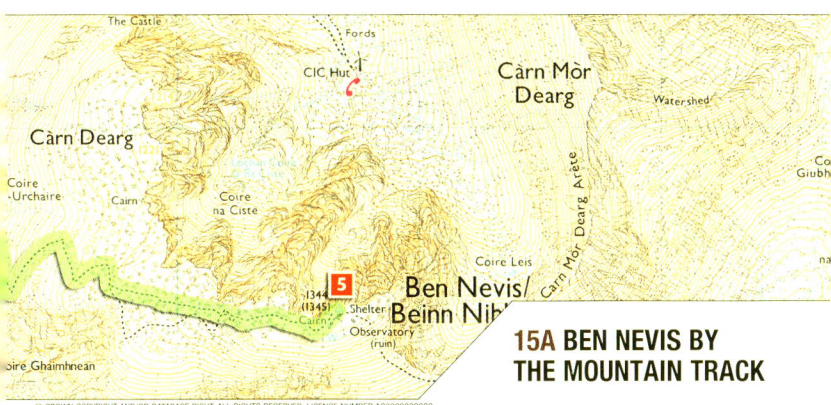

GLEN NEVIS VISITOR CENTRE

15A BEN NEVIS BY THE MOUNTAIN TRACK

Directions – Ben Nevis by the Mountain Track continued...

3 **Turn sharp left** on the main path to avoid a very eroded and unpleasant branch path straight ahead. The route soon leads up to the plateau of Lochan Meall an t-Suidhe, also known as the halfway lochan – an optimistic nickname as there is still more than half the height to climb. Stay on the path which keeps well to the right of the lochan and arrive at a path junction.

4 **Turn right** then continue along the path; after 500m cross the Red Burn which cascades across the path. **Continue climbing**, following the path which becomes rockier and rougher as it continues uphill. **Follow the zigzags** to avoid increasing the erosion. Higher up the path keeps above the steep scree of Coire Ghaimhnean to your right; these slopes lead to Five Finger Gully, the scene of many fatalities. Particularly when descending, many people steer away from the north face in poor visibility and end up too far south, instead veering into the gully. Consider this and don't allow yourself to become a statistic. In good weather the views down to Glen Nevis as the summit plateau is approached are superb. **Follow the path** as it flattens off and passes near the top of a gully; look out for climbers coming up Tower Ridge and crossing the notorious Tower Gap below. Just before the summit, pass the top of Gardyloo Gully – named by the weathermen who used to empty their chamber pots down it when they were manning the summit observatory at the end of the nineteenth century. **Keep well back from the face** if there is any snow remaining, as cornices often overhang the edge and can collapse.

5 The large summit plateau has a trig point, numerous cairns and memorials as well as the remains of the observatory. On a clear day the view radiates across much of the Highlands. To return **head back down the outward route**. In poor visibility it is essential to check that you are on the correct route and to steer a safe course between Gardyloo Gully and Five Finger Gully, especially when under snow. In such conditions **follow a bearing of 231 degrees for 150m from the trig point, and then a bearing of 281 degrees**, to pass the most dangerous section.

Follow the path down the zigzags and **cross the Red Burn**. **Turn left** at the junction near the halfway lochan and continue retracting your steps down the lower slopes to eventually return triumphant at the start in Glen Nevis.

LOCHAN MEALL AN T-SUIDHE

CÀRN MÒR DEARG ARÊTE

15b Ben Nevis by the Càrn Mòr Dearg Arête

17.8km/11.1miles

The Ben Nevis route for connoisseurs – this very strenuous route includes a dramatic scramble along an airy ridge with stunning views of the north face.

Torlundy » Allt a' Mhuilinn » Càrn Dearg Meadhonach » Càrn Mòr Dearg » Càrn Mòr Dearg Arête » Ben Nevis » Lochan Meall an t-Suidhe » Allt a' Mhuilinn » Torlundy

Start
North Face car park, Torlundy, off the A82 north-east of Fort William. GR: NN 145764.

The Walk
For fit, experienced and confident hillwalkers the narrow arête linking the mountains of Càrn Mòr Dearg and Ben Nevis is one of the finest ridges in Britain and a fabulous approach to our highest summit.

Starting from the North Face car park the route climbs through forest before following the tumbling Allt a' Mhuilinn, and then across the broad flank of Càrn Beag Dearg. Boggy at first, the going soon improves and after a long, tough climb the ridge is reached just before the minor summit of Càrn Dearg Meadhonach. From here a glorious section of ridge links to the sharp peak which gives the upcoming arête its name – Càrn Mòr Dearg. The view of Ben Nevis and the connecting ridge from here is unforgettable.

The arête offers fairly easy scrambling over mainly large blocks of stone but it's very exposed and in poor weather or icy conditions can be a very serious undertaking. A bypass path on the left provides an alternative on some sections but this is also exposed and requires care. For the confident this stretch of rock-hopping among some of the most spectacular scenery in Scotland will be a highlight. At the far end a steep, rocky climb leads directly to the summit plateau of the Ben.

From the summit, extreme care is needed to ensure the correct route down is reached as there are dangerous gullies on both sides. In poor visibility excellent map and compass skills are required to get past this section. Beyond it the stony path zigzags all the way down to the Red Burn. After passing the halfway lochan a rough descent leads to a crossing of the Allt a' Mhuilinn and a return back through the forest.

BEN NEVIS BY THE CÀRN MÒR DEARG ARÊTE

DISTANCE: 17.8KM/11.1MILES » **TOTAL ASCENT:** 1,539M/5,049FT » **START GR:** NN 145764 » **TIME:** ALLOW 10.5 HOURS **SATNAV:** PH33 6SW » **MAP:** OS EXPLORER 392, BEN NEVIS & FORT WILLIAM, 1:25,000 » **REFRESHMENTS:** THE BRIDGE CAFE, SPEAN BRIDGE, OR THE WILDCAT, FORT WILLIAM » **NAVIGATION:** GOOD NAVIGATION AND MOUNTAIN EXPERIENCE REQUIRED.

Directions – Ben Nevis by the Càrn Mòr Dearg Arête

S The Forestry and Land Scotland North Face car park is signed from the A82 a few kilometres north-east of Fort William, accessed via a track from Torlundy. To begin the walk, **take the track** past the vehicle barrier and when the track curves left **turn right** on to a path, signed *North Face Trail*. **Go straight ahead** at a junction with the Puggy Line Trail, then **keep right** on the main path at a fork. The path now winds uphill. Continue ahead when a smaller path joins from the left. Soon a bench is passed with views over the head of Loch Linnhe and along Loch Eil. At the next junction **keep right,** signed for the *North Face and CIC Hut*. Pass a picnic table with another superb view. When a track is reached, with a bridge on the right, **go straight ahead** up the track, soon passing a hydro dam. At a track junction **turn right**. At the top of the forestry the track ends. **Cross the stile** to follow the path up the east side of the Allt a' Mhuilinn.

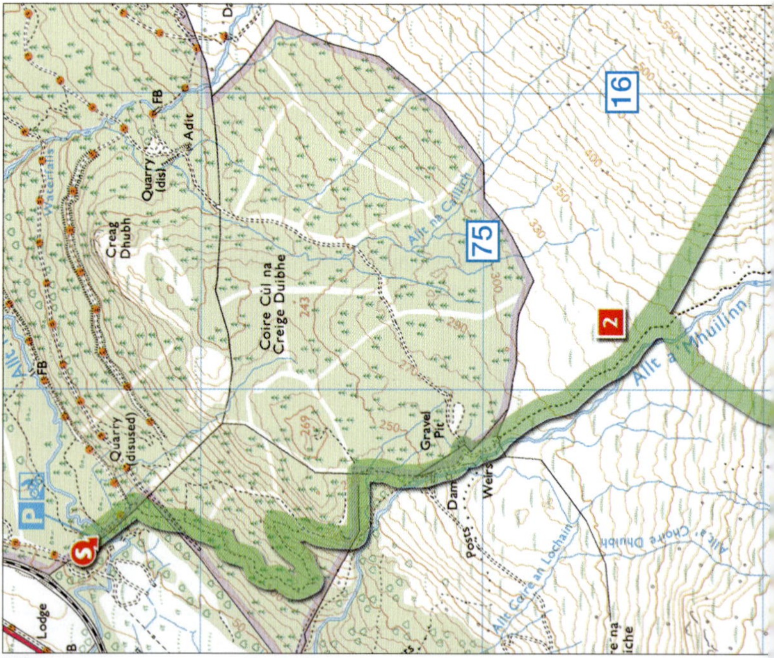

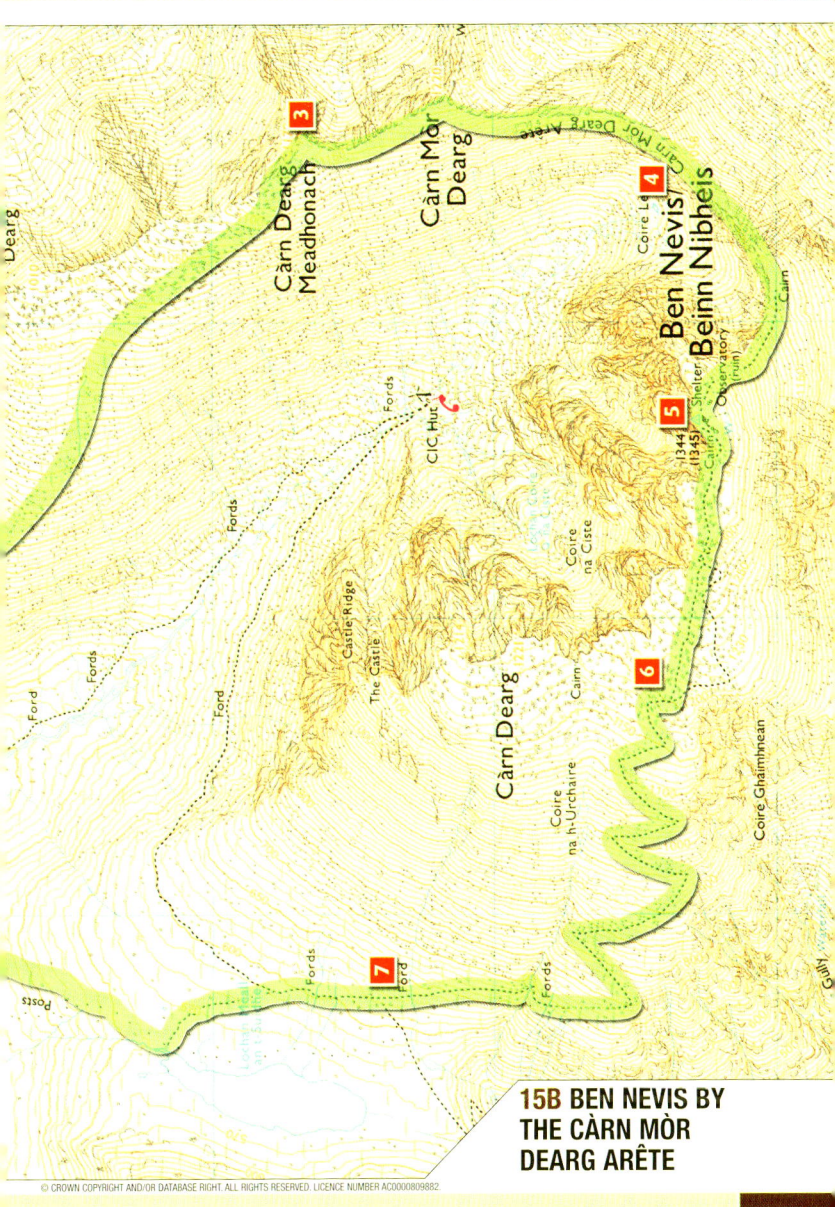

15B BEN NEVIS BY THE CÀRN MÒR DEARG ARÊTE

Directions – Ben Nevis by the Càrn Mòr Dearg Arête continued...

2 **At a fork turn left** on to a much smaller path. The path can be boggy in places at first but soon improves. **Continue climbing across the slopes** and enjoy the fabulous views to the cliffs and gullies of the north face of the Ben opposite, aiming to join the ridge at the summit of Càrn Dearg Meadhonach.

3 **Continue along the ridge** to reach the pointed peak of Càrn Mòr Dearg, at 1,220m the first Munro of the day. From here the stunning rocky arête curves gracefully to link with the final slopes of Ben Nevis. **Descend** on loose ground to start your progress along it. **Follow the crest of the ridge**; this involves fairly easy scrambling over large blocks. It is possible to bypass parts of the arête using a path on the left, but care is needed as this is also exposed; the crest itself may provide surer footing. The surroundings are spectacular. **Climb to a minor peak** and follow the arête as it curves right. **Stay on the ridge** and descend to the low point.

4 **Climb again,** soon crossing the narrowest section of the arête. A further ascent leads to a brief flattening before a cairn marks the start of the final ascent of Ben Nevis. **Head directly up** the boulders and pick up short sections of path among the scree to reach the summit plateau.

5 A trig point marks the summit; there are also a number of cairns and the remains of the observatory built in 1883 and used for over twenty years. **Descend from the summit plateau** via the main Mountain Track. In clear weather this is straightforward to find but in low cloud or when there is snow on the ground **very careful navigation is required** in order to find the safe line off the plateau. There have been numerous accidents and fatalities over the years as walkers have failed to navigate a safe route between Gardyloo Gully and Five Finger Gully. In such conditions **follow a bearing of 231 degrees for 150m from the trig point and then a bearing of 281 degrees**, to pass the most dangerous section.

6 **Continue down** the large rocky path as it zigzags downhill, accompanied by a stream of walkers on fair summer days. Eventually **cross the Red Burn** and soon reach a path junction.

7 Continue straight ahead, ignoring the main path to the left; at the next path junction **fork left** on to a well-made path to reach the outflow of Lochan Meall an t-Suidhe, also known as the halfway lochan. From here **leave the path and aim north-north-east** down over tussocky rough ground aiming for the Allt a' Mhuilinn. There are normally a few easy places to cross, but if in spate head downstream, over a deer fence at a stile and follow a rough path to a bridge. Otherwise **cross the water** and head up the other side of the burn to join the outward route; **turn left** along it to retrace the route back down to Torlundy.

SUMMIT CLIFFS OF BEN NEVIS

STOB COIRE EASAIN

16 The Grey Corries

21.1km/13.1miles

This major mountain walk takes in three Munros on one of the most distinctive ridges in Scotland.

Parking south of Coire Choille » Stob Coire Gaibhre » Stob Choire Claurigh » Stob Coire an Laoigh » Stob Coire Easain » Sgùrr Choinnich Mòr » Stob Coire Easain » An Socach » Parking south of Coire Choille

Start

Take the minor road east from Spean Bridge railway station and from Coire Choille follow a very rough track for 1.7km to a parking area where another track branches right. GR: NN 253793.

The Walk

This fine ridge of quartzite-clad peaks is well seen in the view from the Commando Memorial at Spean Bridge, and offers a classic mountain walk. The circuit described here takes in three of the Munros of The Grey Corries, leaving the outlying peak of Stob Bàn for baggers to claim on another day. Once the initial slog of an ascent is out of the way, a superb ridge traverse lies ahead. The route is best saved for good weather to get a full sense of the majesty of this complex terrain.

Leaving Coire Choille, the walk follows a track to begin with. Walkers are soon greeted by the slightly spooky outstretched hand of the Wee Minister. This wooden statue, thought to represent Dr Thomas Chalmers (or possibly a later Moderator of the Free Church of Scotland, the Reverend John McIntosh), replaced an earlier stone statue that originally stood in the grounds of Fort William Manse before it was moved to this position during World War I. Said to bring good luck to passers by, people traditionally left coins in the minister's hand. Nowadays a box for donations to the local mountain rescue team sits at the minister's feet.

Soon the route leaves the track for a brutally steep ascent up pathless ground before easier going leads to the ridge proper. From here the route onwards is a delightful long ridgewalk picking off the first two Munros before an out and back detour to Sgùrr Choinnich Mòr, the third Munro of the day, which can be omitted if time or energy are short. The descent is straightforward at first, with many a satisfying glance back over the ridge completed, before awkward boggy and grassy ground leads to a short section of forestry and a final march along tracks back to the start.

THE GREY CORRIES

DISTANCE: 21.1KM/13.1MILES » **TOTAL ASCENT:** 1,547M/5,075FT » **START GR:** NN 253793 » **TIME:** ALLOW 10 HOURS **SATNAV:** PH34 4EY » **MAP:** OS EXPLORER 392, BEN NEVIS & FORT WILLIAM, 1:25,000 » **REFRESHMENTS:** THE BRIDGE CAFE, SPEAN BRIDGE » **NAVIGATION:** RIDGE WALKING FOR MUCH OF THE ROUTE; SOME PATHLESS SECTIONS; GOOD NAVIGATION SKILLS AND HILLWALKING EXPERIENCE REQUIRED.

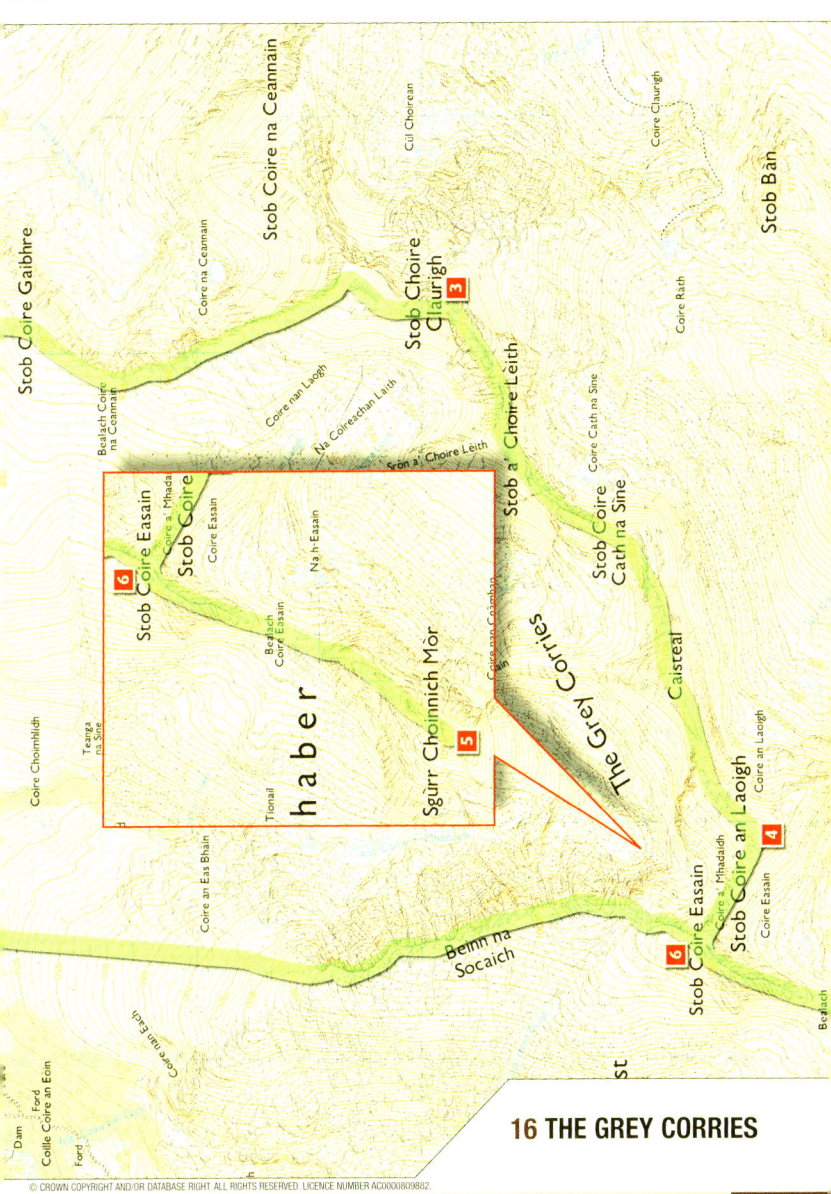

16 THE GREY CORRIES

Directions – The Grey Corries

1 The parking area is several kilometres along a very rough track from Coire Choille – great care is needed to protect your vehicle's suspension. Begin walking where another track branches right, **follow the track ahead** in a southeasterly direction. **Go through a gate**, and try not to be spooked by the Wee Minister. **Keep heading uphill**, passing through blocks of forestry. At the end of the trees on the right, **go through the gate** and stay on the track.

2 Go through a second gate, then **immediately turn right** to cross wet, pathless ground, keeping the fence on your right as you **climb steeply**. When the gradient eases, **traverse south-west** across the slope before aiming **more directly south** to climb the long slope leading to Stob Coire Gaibhre. Here the superb ridge walking begins, and epic views are revealed over the tiny lochan nestling in the corrie of the outlying summit Stob Coire na Ceannain on your left. **Descend briefly then climb** gradually at first and then more steeply over rocky ground to a high point at 1,121m. **Climb steeply ahead** to reach the narrow crest leading to Stob Choire Claurigh. There are bypass paths if you want to avoid the ridge. Marked by a cairn, this is the first Munro of the day and the fifteenth highest mountain in Britain; it offers an enticing view of the ridge to come.

3 **Descend the stony, broad ridge** (a path helps); after passing over a minor bump the ridge narrows and becomes grassier. **Climb over stony ground** to reach a rocky crest with steep crags on your left to reach the minor summit of Stob Coire Cath na Sine. The ridge now heads more directly west. Cross another stony area and **climb to the high point of Caisteal** at 1,106m. From here **continue along the sinuous ridge** to reach Stob Coire an Laoigh which has impressive tiered crags on the right and is the second Munro of the walk.

4 **Descend stony ground and then climb** to reach the summit of Stob Coire Easain at 1,080m. At this point it is possible to miss out the third Munro, Sgùrr Choinnich Mòr, by heading down the north-east ridge described in stage 6. However for those intent on bagging the Munros this would leave a longish day walk to climb a single peak (though the approach along Glen Nevis is beautiful). To include the peak, **head south-south-west** down the clear ridge to the wide Bealach Coire Easain. **Climb very steeply** and then **follow the well-defined ridge** up the pyramid-shaped peak of Sgùrr Choinnich Mòr.

5 At 1,094m this is the third Munro of the day. **Return to the bealach** and then back up to Stob Coire Easain.

6 From here **take the north-east ridge,** heading down steep, stony ground at first before the gradient eases and the going becomes grassier underfoot. A number of minor peaks are passed as the ridge heads over Beinn na Socaich. There are great views back behind you of The Grey Corries. As the slope becomes more grassy and open, **aim north-north-east** over increasingly boggy and tussocky ground. **Aim for a gate in the forest fence** and **follow a faint path** through the trees. **Stay on the improving path**, soon reaching a forest track.

7 **Turn right** along the forest track. **Cross a bridge** and ignore a track to the left, instead continue ahead to a T-junction. **Turn left** downhill. Stay on the main track and **turn right** at the next junction (*Spean Bridge* is signed straight ahead). Ignore another track to the left but **branch left downhill** at the next junction to return to the start.

STOB COIRE NA CEANNAIN

SECTION 4

The Road to the Isles

The Road to the Isles extends north-west from Fort William, eventually leading to the fishing port of Mallaig. This is one of Scotland's most scenic routes, with both a road and the famous railway the West Highland Line running through a region of rugged grandeur.

It's an area where history and romance intertwine. At Glenfinnan a great monument commemorates Bonnie Prince Charlie's uprising in a setting of incomparable scenic beauty, while the spectacular railway viaduct has become famous through the Harry Potter films. Further on the great mountains give way to an equally stunning coastline around Arisaig. Beyond, the gleaming Silver Sands of Morar featured in the classic film Local Hero.

LOOKING NORTH FROM THE ARDNISH PENINSULA

PEANMEANACH BEACH

17 Peanmeanach

11.3km/7miles

Rugged moorland walk leading to a beautiful wild beach and abandoned village.

Polnish » Railway » Loch Doire a' Ghearrain » Oakwoods » Peanmeanach » Oakwoods » Loch Doire a' Ghearrain » Railway » Polnish

Start

Lay-by at Polnish on A830 between Lochailort railway station and Beasdale railway station, just north of Loch Dubh. GR: NM 742835.

The Walk

This surprisingly rugged walk heads through a variety of different habitats to reach the stunning beach and the ruins of an abandoned village at Peanmeanach. Back in 1841 the seven houses here were home to forty-eight people, the population having been swelled by those fleeing here from the Highland Clearances elsewhere, forced on to poorer land that could ill support so many. The last resident, Nellie MacQueen, left in 1942 when paraffin – the only source of light – was rationed; her home became a mountain bothy for many years but closed to the public in 2020 and is now a privately rented cottage.

The walk follows the line of the original path to the village, once maintained by two 'road-builders' at the expense of Ardnish residents. Starting from a lay-by on the Road to the Isles, the path soon leads to a bridge over the railway and then across rough and boggy ground to climb up to a small ridge. From here there are fabulous views of the numerous islands dotted in the surrounding sea lochs; if you are lucky you might even glimpse a white-tailed eagle, Britain's largest bird of prey.

After crossing the moors the path leads down through a beautiful section of ancient oakwood. From here a flat area of wet ground leads to the ruined village of Peanmeanach. The former bothy is now private and kept locked; note the rounded corners of the walls on some of the older blackhouses.

Just a short walk beyond is the beach, an enchanting spot to while away an hour, with expanses of shell sand and shingle. It is frequently visited by kayakers. There's a hidden beach just around the headland to explore before retracing your steps over the moor.

PEANMEANACH

DISTANCE: 11.3KM/7MILES » **TOTAL ASCENT:** 395M/1,296FT » **START GR:** NM 742835 » **TIME:** ALLOW 4.5 HOURS
SATNAV: PH38 4NA » **MAP:** OS EXPLORER 398, LOCH MORAR & MALLAIG, 1:25,000 » **REFRESHMENTS:** LOCHAILORT INN, LOCHAILORT, OR CAFE RHU, ARISAIG » **NAVIGATION:** PATHS OFTEN BOGGY; ROUTE FINDING CAN BE TRICKY.

Directions – Peanmeanach

1 **Go through the gap in the fence** from the lay-by on the seaward side of the A830, signed for *Peanmeanach*. **Pass to the left** of a small gravel quarry, and **head downhill** on the often wet path, passing through birch woods. **Cross the bridge** over the railway. This is the Fort William to Mallaig line, on which The Jacobite steam train runs in the summer months.

2 Stay on the path and **cross a wooden footbridge**. **Branch left** at a fork to head uphill over rough ground to reach the top of a small crest. From here there are stunning views along the coastline. **Descend briefly** and then climb on to a ridge overlooking Loch Beag. This sea loch opens out into Loch nan Uamh, where Bonnie Prince Charlie landed during the Jacobite rebellion of 1745. His departure the following year from the same area is commemorated by a large cairn just a short way round the coast beside the road near Cuildarrach. The path becomes drier underfoot as it crosses the moor, and fabulous views to the small isles of Rùm and Eigg are revealed ahead.

3 Stay on the path to **pass a burn feeding Loch Doire a' Ghearrain**. If you're lucky you may spot the red throated divers which have made this loch their summer home – as the name suggests look out for the deep red plumage at the throat. **Cross the next burn** on stepping stones and take care to **stay on the main path** which still retains some of its ancient paving as it descends towards the woods.

4 These trees are the remains of old oak woodlands and provide a rare, lichen-encrusted habitat for birds and insects as the path winds downhill to reach a large flat area of moor grass and reeds. The path is easy to make out, **follow it as it cuts a straight route** towards the sea with a couple of very marshy areas to negotiate.

5 The path eventually reaches the remains of the houses of Peanmeanach, a row of stone cottages facing the sea. The last house to be occupied was restored as a bothy for some years but is now private and kept locked.

6 **Cross the springy turf** in front of the cottages to reach the beach. At low tide there's a wide expanse of sand exposed together with mussel-festooned rocks further out – a lovely place for a break and a spot of beachcombing. **Retrace your steps** to return to the start.

17 PEANMEANACH – **THE ROAD TO THE ISLES**

APPROACH TO THE SUMMIT OF GULVAIN

18 Gulvain

21.4km/13.3miles

A long approach up Gleann Fionnlighe is followed by the steep ascent of this isolated solitary Munro, it's twin peaks linked by a fine ridge.

A830 » Gleann Fionnlighe » Na Socachan » Leac a' Chaiginn » Gulvain summit » Leac a' Chaiginn » Na Socachan » Gleann Fionnlighe » A830

Start

Lay-by on the A861, just off the A830 Fort William to Mallaig road near Kinlocheil. GR: NM 960793.

The Walk

Gulvain is a remote and solitary Munro, lying hidden, unseen from roads, ensuring it has remained one of the lesser climbed of the 3,000-foot summits. Its name is an anglicisation of the original Gaelic, Gaor Bheinn, meaning filth or noise. It is possible that the name refers to the barren stony ground on the north side of the mountain, but more likely it is from the autumn roaring from the rutting stags which populate the slopes.

The lengthy approach along Gleann Fionnlighe really enhances the feeling of isolation, passing the remains of long-gone habitation. Beyond it the mountain rises in unremittingly steep but grassy slopes for 700 metres before easing slightly and reaching the first of two false summits. There's a further climb to reach the south top, marked by a trig point. The grand final ridge that leads from here to the true summit, at 987 metres, is the best part of the day, all the sweeter for being hard earned.

Gulvain is the highest mountain in all the wild area between Loch Arkaig and the Road to the Isles. The 360-degree mountain panorama is exceptional; a large cairn provides a resting spot to enjoy the view and contemplate that long, long walk back down the slopes and along the track back to the start.

GULVAIN

DISTANCE: 21.4KM/13.3MILES » **TOTAL ASCENT:** 1,302M/4,272FT » **START GR:** NM 960793 » **TIME:** ALLOW 8 HOURS
SATNAV: PH33 7NP » **MAP:** OS EXPLORER 398, LOCH MORAR & MALLAIG, AND 399, LOCH ARKAIG, 1:25,000
REFRESHMENTS: GLENFINNAN HOUSE HOTEL, GLENFINNAN, OR JJ'S CAFE, LOCHYBRIDGE, NEAR FORT WILLIAM
NAVIGATION: STRAIGHTFORWARD BUT VERY REMOTE; REQUIRES GOOD MAP READING SKILLS AND HILLWALKING EXPERIENCE.

Directions – Gulvain

➲ Start from the lay-by on the A861, just off the A830 near Kinlocheil. **Walk back to and cross the A830; turn right** along the verge and then **turn left on to a driveway. Turn right** at the houses and **cross the bridge** over the Fionn Lighe. **Turn left** on to a track signed for *Strathan*. **Follow the track** as it undulates along the east side of Gleann Fionnlighe for 2km, passing through attractive birchwoods.

2 **Stay on the track** as it returns to the river; **cross the bridge** and continue up the west side of the glen, passing an old cottage and shed and later the abandoned building at Dail nan Uamhachan. From here the track is rougher but still passable on a mountain bike. **Fork right** when the track branches, staying close to the river. The glen opens up once the forest is left behind and you will often see red deer on the surrounding slopes – or hear them rutting in the autumn. **After 2km, cross the Allt a' Choire Rèidh**. The steep slopes of Gulvain can now be seen directly ahead.

3 Soon after crossing the stream **fork right** at a junction marked by a small cairn. Cross the flat ground to reach the base of the mountain and then **bear left** on a sometimes indistinct hill path to begin the climb. **Climb steeply** uphill for a tough 700m; looking back the views improve with every contour line gained. There are zigzags on the steepest sections. **Keep heading straight uphill** as the gradient eases a little to reach the first false summit at 855m.

4 Descend to **pass two small lochans** and climb the broad grass and stony ridge ahead to eventually reach the south summit of Gulvain at 961m.

5 Marked by a trig point and separated not only by a 1km ridge but also on a separate OS Landranger map, some baggers have mistaken this for the summit in poor visibility and returned to the glen from here. However the true summit of Gulvain lies along the lovely curving north-east ridge; walk along the ridge to reach the summit.

6 The remote nature of the peak makes this a wonderful vantage point, with the whole of west Lochaber laid out in all directions. **Retrace your steps** to return to the start.

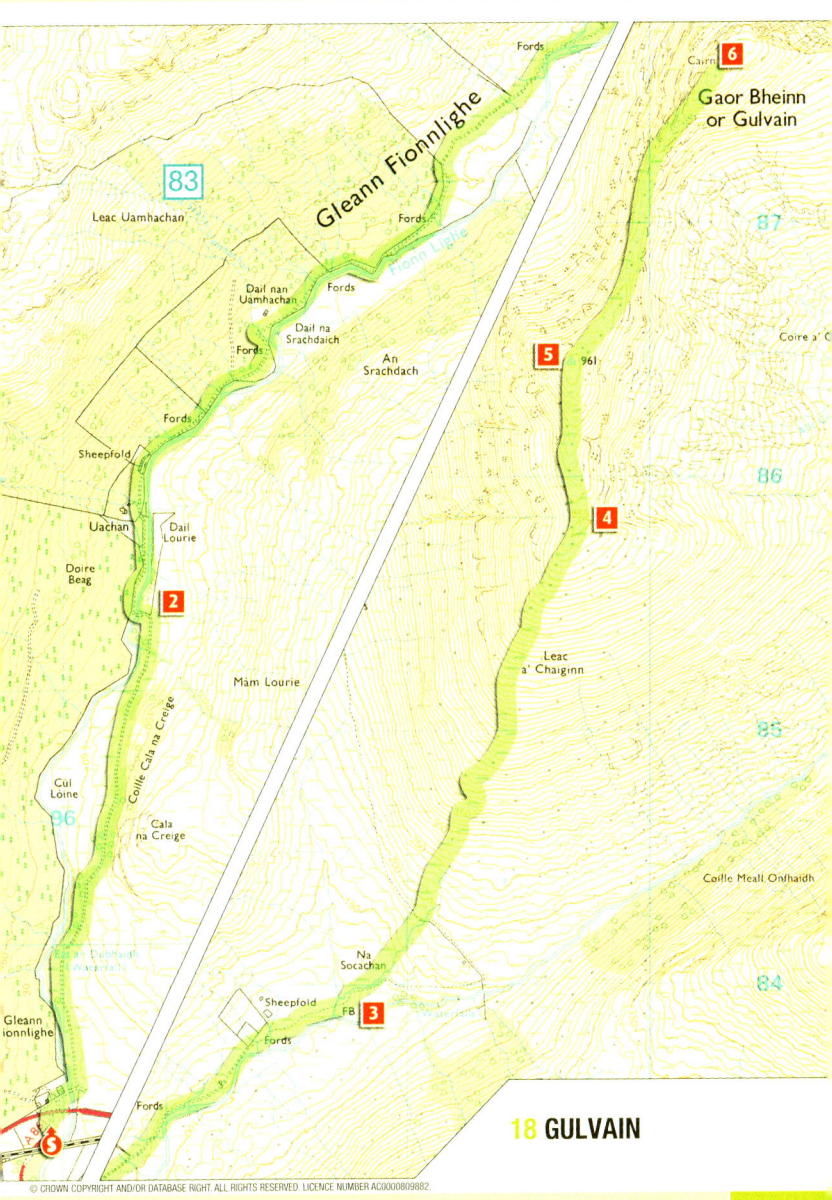

18 GULVAIN

DESCENDING FROM SGÙRR NAN COIREACHAN

19 Sgùrr Thuilm & Sgùrr nan Coireachan

23.2km/14.4miles

This long and demanding mountain hike gives a flavour of the famously rugged terrain of the Rough Bounds of Knoydart.

Glenfinnan » Corryhully Bothy » Druim Coire a' Bheithe » Sgùrr Thuilm » Beinn Gharbh » Sgùrr nan Coireachan » Sgùrr a' Choire Riabhaich » Corryhully Bothy » Glenfinnan

Start
Glenfinnan Visitor Centre (parking charge). GR: NM 907807.

The Walk

These two Munros offer an extremely rugged and strenuous hillwalk of great character, on the fringes of the famous Rough Bounds of Knoydart. It starts by heading along the private road leading up Glen Finnan, soon passing under the huge Glenfinnan Viaduct. As this road is used for the return it is possible to cycle the first four kilometres to Corryhully Bothy and secure a bike there for the way back. On foot there is time to get up close and personal with the thirty-metre-high concrete viaduct, which was completed in 1901. It's become a hugely popular place to visit following its starring role in the Harry Potter films.

The surfaced road is left behind near Corryhully Bothy, and boggier ground is soon encountered as the hillwalk proper begins. The first ascent starts in a fairly brutal fashion, but after gaining height it eases off to follow a lovely grassy ridge, eventually heading up to the summit of Sgùrr Thuilm.

From here there's a fabulous rough and complex ridge which eventually leads to the second Munro, Sgùrr nan Coireachan. Although lower than Sgùrr Thuilm, it's a better viewpoint for this spectacularly remote part of the Highlands.

The descent is long and intricate, following a broad ridge at first. There's some very steep ground before a stalkers' path leads off the ridge and back down into the glen. Now the outward route is retraced back to Glenfinnan. If legs aren't too tired the Glenfinnan Monument, looking out over Loch Shiel, is well worth a visit. It marks the spot where Bonnie Prince Charlie raised the Jacobite standard at the start of the ill-fated 1745 rebellion, which came to a bloody end at Culloden in 1746.

SGÙRR THUILM & SGÙRR NAN COIREACHAN

DISTANCE: 23.2KM/14.4MILES » **TOTAL ASCENT:** 1,413M/4,636FT » **START GR:** NM 907807 » **TIME:** ALLOW 10.5 HOURS
SATNAV: PH37 4LT » **MAP:** OS EXPLORER 398, LOCH MORAR & MALLAIG, 1:25,000 » **REFRESHMENTS:** GLENFINNAN HOUSE HOTEL, GLENFINNAN » **NAVIGATION:** REMOTE PATHLESS MOUNTAIN WALK REQUIRING EXCELLENT NAVIGATION SKILLS AND HILLWALKING EXPERIENCE.

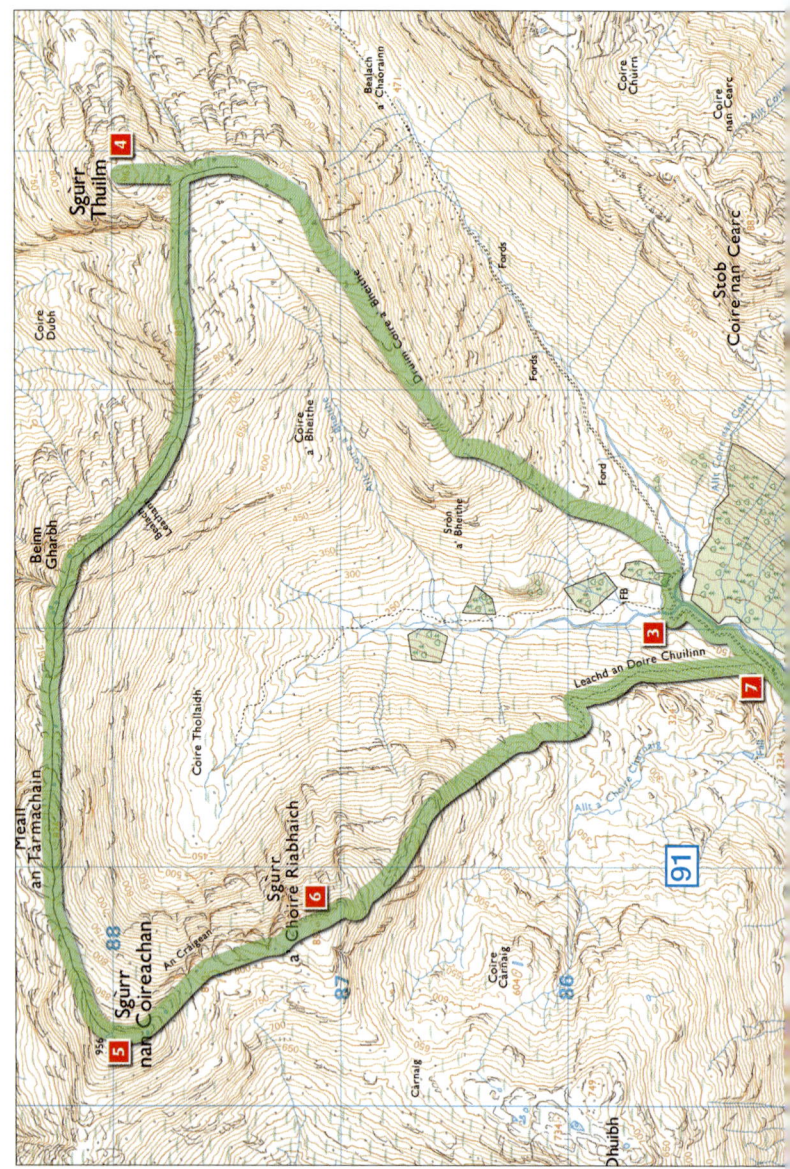

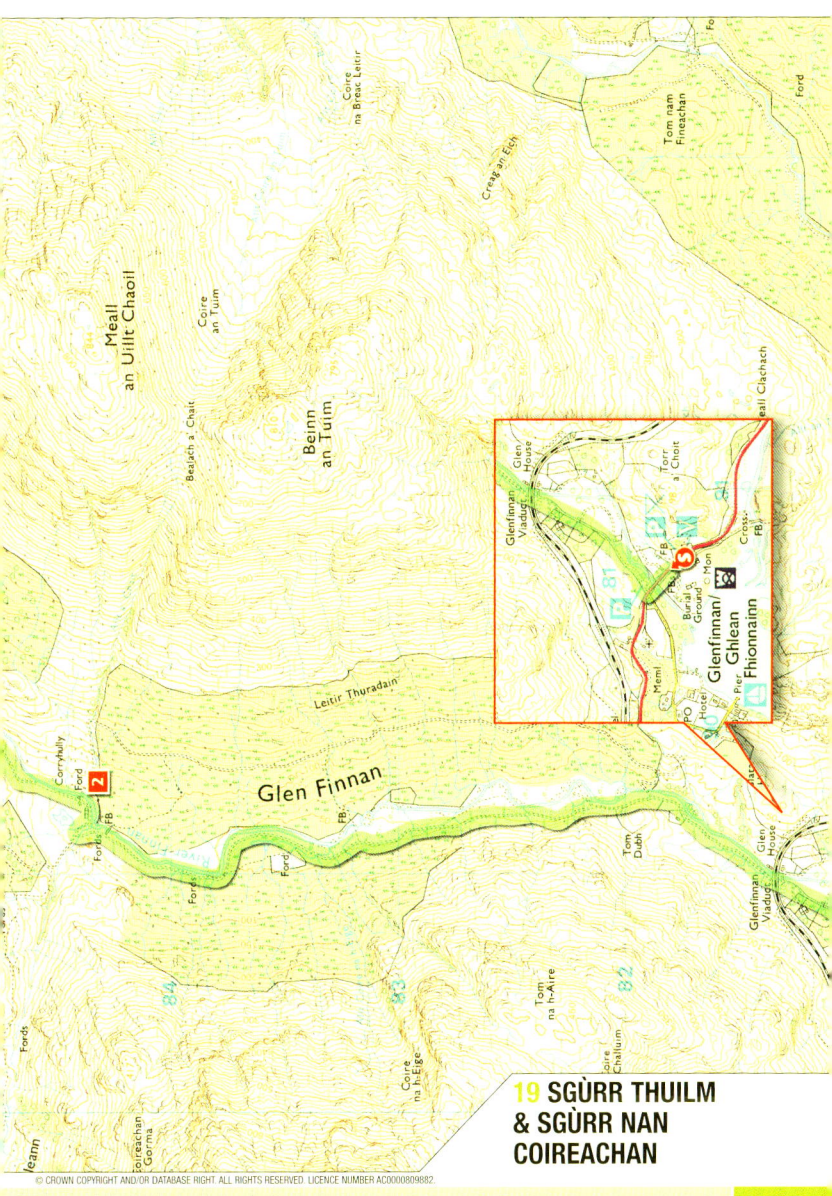

19 SGÙRR THUILM & SGÙRR NAN COIREACHAN

Directions – Sgùrr Thuilm & Sgùrr nan Coireachan

5➤ Begin from the car park at the Glenfinnan Visitor Centre off the A830 Fort William to Mallaig road at Glenfinnan. With both the monument to Bonnie Prince Charlie and the Glenfinnan Viaduct nearby, it gets very busy so it's best to arrive early; there are plans for more car parking across the river. **Turn right** along the main road; cross the bridge over the river and **turn right** immediately to follow a gated track up the glen, soon passing under the impressive Glenfinnan Viaduct. **Keep following the tarmac track** up the glen. After 3km cross the bridge over the Allt a' Chaol-ghlinne, then **bear right** on to a rougher track, leaving the tarmac behind and soon reaching Corryhully Bothy.

2 Probably once a shepherd's cottage, the building is now used by the estate during the stalking season but is available for walkers outside of that time. It makes a useful place for a sheltered break, but please respect it and leave no litter. Beyond the bothy **stay on the track** following the banks of the River Finnan for another 1.5km, keeping straight on at a cross tracks.

3 **Cross a bridge** and continue until you are beyond a patch of trees on the left. Soon after this **turn left onto a faint path,** heading directly for the Druim Coire a' Bheithe ridge. After an initial boggy section the route improves and climbs steep ground to the right of a stream. Above 600m the walking becomes easier as the grassy ridge is followed; there are great views back down the glen. **Bear left,** following the ridge line, go over a small hillock and **follow a line of fence posts for a short time** before leaving these to climb directly to the summit of Sgùrr Thuilm.

4 The cairn marks the higher of the two Munros at 963m. There are good views down remote Loch Arkaig and into Knoydart. To continue to Sgùrr nan Coireachan **walk south to return to the fence posts and then head west,** following the posts on to the winding ridge. The ridge is rough and rocky in places but there is a path for most of it. After the first small top **head down** to the lowest point on the ridge before **climbing to another minor top. Descend again** before climbing to reach Beinn Gharbh. From here the conditions underfoot are much rockier. **Pass a small lochan** and continue to the final minor summit, Meall an Tàrmachain. **Head downhill briefly** before tackling the **final climb** to the summit of Sgùrr nan Coireachan, enjoying good views to Loch Morar.

5 The trig point marks the 956m high point and makes a great spot for a break to soak in the wild panorama. To descend, **head down the broad south-east ridge**. Fairly soon this rises to the minor summit of Sgùrr a' Choire Riabhaich.

6 From here the ridge becomes very steep, with bands of grass and broken rock. **Bear right** away from the ridge at the top of the steep section to follow a path down eroded ground. **Stay on the path** as it tracks back left and regains the ridge, continuing down to easier ground. Soon it steepens again, but without difficulty. This leads to a broad open slope. Further down, after a rockier section, a clear stalkers' path needs to be picked up; **descend a series of zigzags** on this, leaving the ridge and descending its eastern flank to head down into the glen.

7 At the bottom **turn right** on to the track to return to Corryhully Bothy and eventually all the way back down the glen to Glenfinnan.

GLENFINNAN VIADUCT

THE RIDGE LEADING TO STREAP

20 Streap

18.2km/11.3miles

A demanding ascent of a rugged yet neglected mountain, reaching the summit via a dramatic and airy arête.

Craigag » Gleann Dubh-Lighe Bothy » Meall an Uillt Chaoil » Stob Coire nan Cearc » Streap » Streap Comhlaidh » Gleann Dubh-Lighe Bothy » Craigag

Start
Craigag car park just off the A830, west of the bridge over the Dubh Lighe. GR: NM 930799.

The Walk
Streap is the Gaelic word for climbing – an appropriate moniker for this steep and rugged mountain with a section of exposed ridge. It just misses out on Munro status, ensuring this remains a peak for connoisseurs; Streap concedes nothing to its higher neighbours. A long, low-level approach walk along the glen leads to a strenuous ascent and then a fantastic walk along the ridge dividing Glen Finnan and Gleann Dubh Lighe.

Setting out from the Craigag car park the route heads gently up Gleann Dubh Lighe, passing a fine bothy. The building is maintained by volunteers from the Mountain Bothies Association – please respect this open shelter and carry out any litter you find here. Further up the glen, the woodland is left behind revealing a stunning view of the whole route and the rocky mountain ahead.

The ascent is tough; a punishing climb leading up to the main ridge at Meall an Uillt Chaoil. From here the ridge provides a superb traverse, rocky and full of character, ending with a very fine airy arête that leads unerringly to the highest cairn. The summit of Streap is a place to linger on a fine day to soak in the superb views, with the head of Loch Arkaig and the complex peaks of Knoydart. The route back is over the subsidiary peak of Streap Comhlaidh, then down the unrelentingly steep but grassy south ridge, before picking up the outward route once back down in the glen.

STREAP

DISTANCE: 18.2KM/11.3MILES » **TOTAL ASCENT:** 1,292M/4,239FT » **START GR:** NM 930799 » **TIME:** ALLOW 8.5 HOURS
SATNAV: PH37 4LT » **MAP:** OS EXPLORER 398, LOCH MORAR & MALLAIG, 1:25,000 » **REFRESHMENTS:** GLENFINNAN HOUSE HOTEL, GLENFINNAN » **NAVIGATION:** GOOD NAVIGATION SKILLS NEEDED; STEEP AND PATHLESS REMOTE TERRAIN.

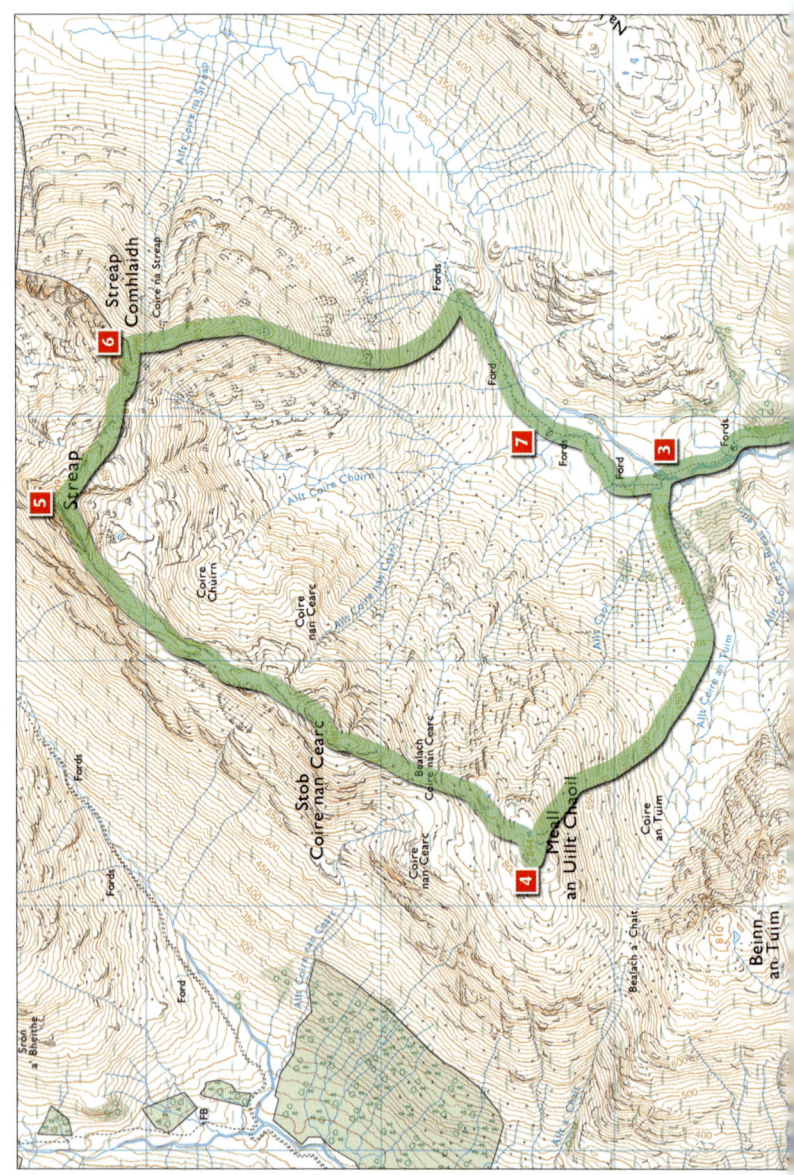

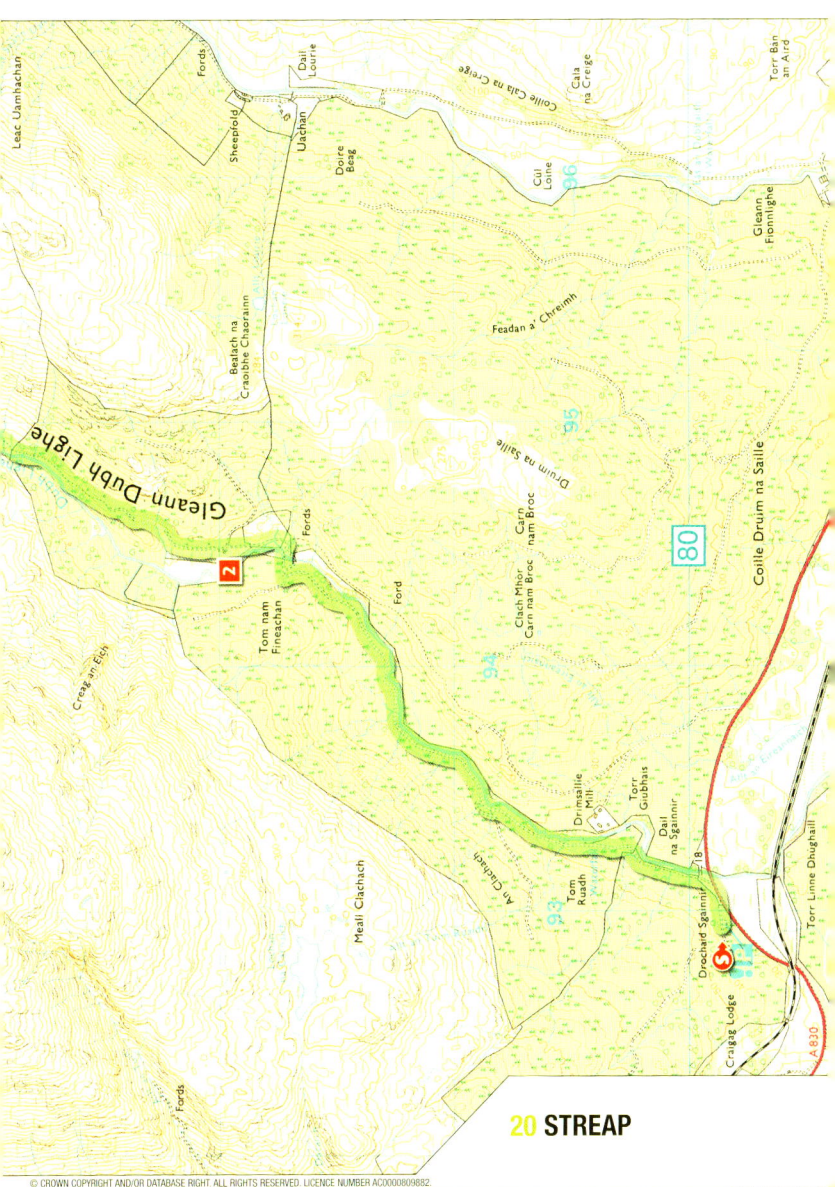

20 **STREAP**

Directions – Streap

S The Craigag car park is on the north side of the A830, 3km east of Glenfinnan and a short distance west of the bridge over the Dubh Lighe. From the car park **head downhill** back to the road and **turn left beside it**, then, before the bridge, **turn left** on to a track. **Go through a gate** and follow the track for 3km along the west bank of the Dubh Lighe. At a junction **turn right** to head downhill and **cross the bridge**. **Follow the track to the left** as it climbs, soon reaching the Gleann Dubh-Lighe Bothy.

2 The lonely stone cottage was gutted by fire in 2011 but has been lovingly restored by volunteers from the Mountain Bothies Association. Please respect it and take your litter home. **Keep on the track and eventually go through a gate**, leaving the trees behind. From this point most of the day's route is in view. The track becomes rougher as it heads up the picturesque glen. **Cross the bridge** back over the Dubh Lighe.

3 **Bear west uphill** on pathless, rough grassy ground; in summer it's best to **stay to the right of a burn** to avoid dense bracken. At the base of Coire an Tuim the gradient eases. **Aim north-west** to stay on the grassy ridge as the terrain steepens again. **Bear west** to join the ridge near the top of Meall an Uillt Chaoil.

4 From the summit **head north–north-east** along the superb ridge. **Keep left on the descent** to the bealach to bypass the rocky outcrops on the ridge. **Climb steeply** to reach the summit of conical Stob Coire nan Cearc, a great vantage point that gives a first view of Streap. **Stay on the ridge, heading downhill** to the next bealach and then **follow the narrow final arête** as it climbs. **Stay on the path** which makes easy work (in summer) of the rocky bands which appeared earlier to block the route.

5 A cairn marks the 909m summit, just 5m short of Munro status. Streap's steep slopes lend great depth to its view, with Loch Arkaig looking particularly impressive from this vantage point. **Aim south-east** to begin the descent, soon following a grassy ridge and reaching a bealach at 818m. From here **climb steeply** to Streap Comhlaidh; there is a faint path for most of the ascent.

6 **Take the south ridge** heading downhill and then climbing to a minor top at 859m. From here **continue downhill**; the descent is steep but mostly grassy – keep to the east of any outcrops. Before the glen floor is reached, **pick up a path** which crosses boggy ground before it meets the Allt Coire Chuirn.

7 **Ford the burn** and **follow the rough path** to reach a ruined building and then rejoin the outward route. **Turn left and cross the bridge** and **follow the track** back down Gleann Dubh Lighe, passing the bothy and crossing the river once more. **Turn left** at the track junction to return to the road. **Turn right** at the road and **turn right again** to reach the car park.

HEADING FOR STREAP COMHLAIDH

Appendix

The following is a list of Visitor Information Centres, shops, cafes, pubs, websites and other contacts that might come in handy.

Visitor Information Centres

Fort William — T: 01397 701 801
Glencoe — T: 01855 811 307

Food & Drink

Cafes

Clachaig Inn, Glen Coe — T: 01855 811 252
Crafts & Things, Glencoe Village — T: 01855 811 325
Glencoe Mountain Resort — T: 01855 851 226
Mo's, Kinlochleven — T: 07425 182 995
JJ's Cafe, Lochybridge — T: 01397 700 532
The Bridge Cafe, Spean Bridge — T: 01397 712 957
The Wildcat, Fort William — T: 01397 698 856

Pubs

Black Isle Bar, Fort William — T: 01397 700 876
Glenfinnan House Hotel, Glenfinnan — T: 01397 601 113
Glen Nevis Restaurant & Bar — T: 01397 705 459
Kingshouse Hotel, Glen Coe — T: 01855 851 259
Lochailort Inn, Lochailort — T: 01687 470 208
The Bothy Bar, Kinlochleven — T: 01855 831 902
The Inn at Ardgour, Corran — T: 01855 841 225

Accommodation
Bed & Breakfast, Hotels and Campsites

www.visitfortwilliam.co.uk
www.visitscotland.com

Hostels & Bunkhouses

www.hostellingscotland.org.uk
www.scottish-hostels.com

Bothies

www.mountainbothies.org.uk

Weather

www.mwis.org.uk
www.metoffice.gov.uk
www.smidgeup.com/midge-forecast

Other Contacts

www.outdooraccess-scotland.scot
www.forestryandland.gov.scot
www.nature.scot/enjoying-outdoors

Outdoor Shops

Ellis Brigham — T: 01397 706 220
Fort William, www.ellis-brigham.com
Cotswold Outdoor — T: 01397 719 118
Fort William, www.cotswoldoutdoor.com
Nevisport — T: 01397 780 011
Fort William, www.nevisport.com

Other Publications

Great Scottish Walks
Helen & Paul Webster, Vertebrate Publishing

Day Walks on the Isle of Skye
Helen & Paul Webster, Vertebrate Publishing

Day Walks in the Cairngorms
Helen & Paul Webster, Vertebrate Publishing

Scottish Island Bagging
Helen & Paul Webster, Vertebrate Publishing

About the Authors

Helen and Paul Webster share a passion for walking and wild places. In 2003–2004 they undertook a life-changing 4,000-mile continuous backpacking trip across Europe. Following their return, they quit their careers to begin a new life evangelising for Scotland's spectacular outdoors – especially the Highlands and Islands. Together they set up Walkhighlands, a free online guide and forum which has become the busiest walkers' website in the UK. They have also written eighteen guidebooks to various areas of Scotland, including *Scottish Island Bagging*, and in 2018 Paul won the Scottish Landscape Photographer of the Year. They live in the Cairngorms National Park.
www.walkhighlands.co.uk

Vertebrate Publishing

At Vertebrate Publishing we publish books to inspire adventure.

It's our rule that the only books we publish are those that we'd want to read or use ourselves. We endeavour to bring you beautiful books that stand the test of time and that you'll be proud to have on your bookshelf for years to come.

The Peak District was the inspiration behind our first books. Our offices are situated on its doorstep, minutes away from world-class climbing, biking and hillwalking. We're driven by our own passion for the outdoors, for exploration, and for the natural world; it's this passion that we want to share with our readers.

We aim to inspire everyone to get out there. We want to connect readers – young and old – with the outdoors and the positive impact it can have on well-being. We think it's particularly important that young people get outside and explore the natural world, something we support through our publishing programme.

As well as publishing award-winning new books, we're working to make available many out-of-print classics in both print and digital formats. These are stories that we believe are unique and significant; we want to make sure that they continue to be shared and enjoyed.
www.adventurebooks.com

DAY WALKS GUIDEBOOKS

Written by local authors, each pocket-sized guidebook features:

- 20 great day-length walks
- Ordnance Survey 1:25,000-scale maps
- easy-to-follow directions
- distance & navigation information
- refreshment stops & local area information
- detailed appendix

1. **DAY WALKS IN THE CAIRNGORMS**
2. **DAY WALKS IN FORT WILLIAM & GLEN COE**
3. **DAY WALKS ON THE ISLE OF SKYE**
4. **DAY WALKS IN SNOWDONIA**
5. **DAY WALKS IN THE BRECON BEACONS**
6. **DAY WALKS ON THE PEMBROKESHIRE COAST**
7. **DAY WALKS IN THE LAKE DISTRICT**
8. **DAY WALKS IN NORTHUMBERLAND**
9. **DAY WALKS IN THE YORKSHIRE DALES**
10. **DAYS WALKS IN THE NORTH YORK MOORS**
11. **DAY WALKS IN THE SOUTH PENNINES**
12. **DAY WALKS IN THE PEAK DISTRICT**
13. **DAY WALKS IN THE PEAK DISTRICT**
14. **DAY WALKS IN THE COTSWOLDS**
15. **DAY WALKS IN DEVON**
16. **DAY WALKS IN CORNWALL**
17. **DAY WALKS ON THE HIGH WEALD**
18. **DAY WALKS ON THE SOUTH DOWNS**

Available from book shops or direct from:
www.adventurebooks.com